" **CORONER** is . . .

FASCINATING . . . CAPTIVATING . . .
Noguchi can finally, and for the first time,
reveal the full facts behind some of his most
compelling and famous cases . . ."
— *Houston Chronicle*

"Here's a medical examiner who out-Quin-
cies TV's Qunicy . . . very readable . . .
NOGUCHI TELLS ALL IN *CORONER*."
— *Minneapolis Tribune*

"Noguchi comes across . . . as a strongly
opinionated man committed to elevating the
practice of forensic pathology . . . enlighten-
ing . . . readers will be waiting to hear his
views on the sensational cases . . . A GOLD-
MINE FOR CELEBRITY WATCHERS."
— *Kirkus Reviews*

"Noguchi has produced an intellectually
challenging work that retains the reader's interest until the end . . . FASCINATING."
— *Atlanta Constitution*

CORONER

THOMAS T. NOGUCHI, M.D.

WITH JOSEPH DiMONA

PUBLISHED BY POCKET BOOKS NEW YORK

POCKET BOOKS, a division of Simon & Schuster, Inc.
1230 Avenue of the Americas, New York, N.Y. 10020

ISBN: 0-671-54088-2

First Pocket Books printing November, 1984

10 9 8 7 6 5 4 3 2 1

I dedicate this book
to my father, Dr. Wataru Noguchi,
and my mother, Tomika.

And to my fellow members of the
National Association of Medical Examiners.

Contents

Contents

Preface

In my memory, as I write, there is a montage of tragic scenes. The body of the beautiful Marilyn Monroe, her hand outstretched in death toward the telephone by her bed. Robert F. Kennedy, so vibrant and active in life, felled by an assassin's bullet in a hotel kitchen. The grim scene at the secluded estate in Bel-Air where the pregnant Sharon Tate lay brutally massacred. The wastebasket in the hotel room where Janis Joplin met her death. The charred ruins of a little house in Los Angeles where the kidnappers of Patty Hearst perished in a hail of police bullets and a raging fire. The bizarre evidence at the scene of Albert Dekker's "suicide." The luxurious—and strangely tidy—apartment in which William Holden was discovered four days after he had died. The red down jacket that Natalie Wood wore when her body was found in the rain-swept waters off Catalina Island. The tiny pinpoints of blood on John Belushi's arm that revealed he had not died of a heart attack.

Because my jurisdiction as Chief Medical Examiner/Coroner of the County of Los Angeles included the motion picture capital, Hollywood, my professional career has been highlighted by famous and controversial cases—controversies that persist even today. Did Marilyn Monroe commit suicide or were the drugs that killed her injected into her body by someone else? Did Sirhan Sirhan or another gunman fire the bullet which killed Robert Kennedy? Could the knives used in the murder of Sharon Tate be identified and traced to the Manson gang if they were never found? What were the real circumstances behind the drug-related death of Janis Joplin? Were the kidnappers of Patty Hearst victims of police brutality or of their own revolutionary zeal? How and why did Albert Dekker and William Holden die? How did Natalie Wood spend the last terrifying moments of her life? Was John Belushi murdered?

I conducted the forensic investigations of each of these cases. It was my job, as mandated by law, to establish the "manner, cause and circumstance" of death and to report my findings to the press and the public. But until now I have been unable to tell the full story behind my investigations. I am writing about them here from my own point of view as a coroner, not only to shed new light on the many troublesome questions that still remain, but to describe the techniques and goals of the little-known profession of forensic medicine itself.

In every death, there is a mystery until the cause is

known. Was it natural or unnatural, a homicide, a suicide, an accident? A coroner is, if you will, a medical detective who is specifically trained to solve that mystery. He supervises the collection of evidence and interviews with witnesses at the scene. He is in charge of the autopsy on the body. And from other forensic specialists he assembles laboratory reports of the presence of minute bits of fiber or metal, the telltale traces of trauma in human tissue, and the characteristics of bone fragments, teeth, blood and body fluids— not only to determine the cause of death, but also to establish the identity of an unknown victim and, sometimes, of the person or persons who may have murdered him. Among my other cases, my staff and I were called upon to identify the badly burned and dismembered casualties of the disastrous collision of a jet airliner and a fighter plane. In a lucky flash of intuition, I was able to determine the cause of death of a young Hollywood actress who appeared to have been shot by a nonexistent bullet. And more than once I was able to uncover evidence of murder in so-called "perfect crimes."

Forensic medicine has always been a fascinating and challenging profession for me. For I believe that every coroner performs a very necessary service both for his community and for society as a whole. I also strongly believe in the independence of the coroner's office as a safeguard for the people. A coroner must be gutsy. His statements and rulings may not always be popular, but he must stand firm in his conviction and tell it as it is.

In every death there are lessons to be learned for the living. Teaching those lessons and translating them into laws are the heart of the coroner's work. And where death stubbornly remains a mystery, we are guided by the thought expressed in a *haiku* I wrote not long ago:

法医学
道なき道を
歩みつつ
トーマス・野口

The principle of forensic medicine.
There is no road to follow.
It is up to us to carve a new road.

CORONER

1

Medical Examiner's Case No. 81-15167

Natalie Wood

Santa Catalina is an island thirty miles out in the ocean, off the southern coast of California. About twenty-two miles long and eight miles wide, it is renowned for its spectacular beauty. The spurs and canyons which radiate from its mountain ridges carve picturesque coves in which sailboats and yachts anchor beneath cliffs. Avalon, on the island's southern tip, is a small community of a few thousand year-round residents, its lovely bay known to be perfect for sailing and for scuba diving, and there are glass-bottomed boats plying the harbor, through which marine life is studied. This is the area of Catalina which most tourists know.

Yachtsmen prefer the more isolated cove at the northern end of the island. In Isthmus Bay, where the mountains swoop straight down to the sea, there are no hotels or accommodations for tourists, and only one bar/restaurant ashore, Doug's Harbor Reef, a favorite meeting place for the sailors whose boats are anchored in the cove. On the night of November 28, 1981, Natalie Wood, her husband Robert Wagner, and actor Christopher Walken, their guest on that long Thanksgiving weekend, dined at Doug's Harbor Reef and then returned to spend the night on *Splendour,* the Wagners' yacht. In the early hours of the following morning, the body of Natalie Wood was found floating, face down, in the sea.

By a strange twist of chance, a deputy on the staff of the Los Angeles County Medical Examiner's Office, our chief consultant on ocean accidents, Paul Miller, was the captain of a schooner moored to the same buoy in front of the Wagners' yacht the night of the tragedy. Miller, a friend of the Wagners', was an Annapolis graduate, president of the California Sailing Academy at Marina Del Rey, one of the largest such schools in the world, and a man who knew intimately the dangerous waters around Catalina Island.

Perhaps never in my experience had the Medical Examiner's Office dealt with a more perfectly positioned expert at the scene of an accident. On that terrible night, Miller dined at the same restaurant as the Wagners and Christopher Walken. After dinner, he returned to his sailing ship half an hour before the Wagners' party, and was on deck when the actors passed by on their way back to *Splendour.* And later that night, it was he who first responded to Wagner's call for assistance.

By another strange coincidence, three years earlier, in 1978, Miller had invited me on a fact-finding mission aboard his schooner. That mission began on the same holiday weekend, Thanksgiving, and in the same bay in which Natalie Wood would perish.

Forensic scientists, as a function of their duties to the public, must explore all the environments of death, for in our profession we deal not only with homicides by gunshot and knife, but with accidents and disasters of every kind on land, at sea and in the air. Drowning fatalities were particularly numerous in Los Angeles, due to the popularity of scuba diving, surfing and sailing. And I had contacted Miller because I wanted to learn more about the factors which contribute to underwater accidents.

During my trip to Catalina, I dined at Doug's Harbor Reef, and as I traveled back to Miller's schooner that evening I noticed something that would become important to my understanding of how and why Natalie Wood died. From many of the boats anchored in the cove, hi-fi music blared across the water, along with the raucous sound of parties. Because of the enveloping noise, only two people, Marilyn Wayne and a friend, who were on a nearby boat, would hear Natalie Wood's anguished cries for help the night she died. By bad luck, they said, a party was being celebrated on a sailing ship close by *Splendour*, with loud rock music echoing across the waves. More poignantly, they reported that they heard Natalie Wood's cries, but didn't try to help because her pleas were answered by people on the deck of that party boat, who called out to her several times, "We're coming to get you."

Even Miller, in the cabin of his sailing ship moored right in front of *Splendour*, didn't hear Natalie Wood, also because of party noise. And, most significantly, Wagner and Walken, on the very ship from which she fell, said they remembered no cries.

As soon as I heard of Natalie Wood's death, I asked Miller for a special investigative report. When it was forwarded to me, I was able to match his expert findings with my own knowledge of the dangerous waters around that windswept little island far out at sea. Our investigations received wide publicity, but part of the story of Natalie Wood's last moments has never been told.

In 1955, three young actors appeared in a motion picture which transformed them, overnight, into major stars. The movie was *Rebel Without a Cause,* featuring James Dean, Sal Mineo and Natalie Wood.

All three of these young actors would suffer untimely deaths. Dean was killed in a highway crash while driving his Porsche to Salinas to compete in a racing event in the same year as the picture's release. (*Giant* would be distributed after his death.) Sal Mineo was stabbed to death in the driveway beside his Hollywood home in 1976. And Natalie Wood perished in a mysterious drowning accident in 1981.

If ever there was a child of Hollywood, it was she. Born Natasha Gurdin in San Francisco on July 20, 1938, she was earning a thousand dollars a week at 20th Century–Fox as early as the age of eight, appearing in such films as *Tomorrow Is Forever* and *Miracle on 34th Street.* In *Rebel Without a Cause* she played her first adult role, and audiences around America reacted enthusiastically both to her beauty and to her sensitive portrayal of a troubled teenager. In Hollywood, her peers in the motion picture industry nominated her for an Academy Award for her performance in the picture.

Later in her career, she would be honored with two more Oscar nominations, for *Splendor in the Grass* in 1961 and *Love With the Proper Stranger* in 1963. And the year before she died, this amazing actress was still on the rise. She was voted the Golden Globe Award as the best actress of 1980, no less than twenty-five years after her first starring role and thirty-nine years after her first movie.

For many Americans, Natalie Wood exemplified the legendary movie actress who dwells in what *The New York Times* called "the Hollywood of celluloid images, mansions and yachts, midnight swims and motorcycle rides, celebrity parties and night life." But in fact her personal life was relatively subdued. She married a handsome young actor, Robert Wagner, in 1957 and divorced him in 1962. Then, after a brief marriage to Richard Gregson, an English film producer, she remarried Wagner in 1972 and remained his wife until her death.

It was, by most accounts, an idyllic marriage of two working actors, rare in Hollywood. Both enjoyed professional success, but their union remained unscarred by the usual envy which undermines most such marriages. They were very much in love and delighted in their children, Katherine, who was sixteen in 1981, Natasha, eleven, and Courtney Broome, seven.

Their marriage was enhanced by another love: the sea. And recently their lives had revolved around *Splendour*, on which they spent most of their week-ends and holidays. Natalie Wood, contrary to some reports, did not seem afraid of the water at all. Fellow sailors often saw her skimming around the harbor alone in the little rubber dinghy that served as a tender for the yacht.

In 1981, as the Thanksgiving holiday weekend approached, both Wagners were, as usual, enjoying professional success. Robert Wagner, known as R.J. to his friends, was co-starring with Stephanie Powers in a highly rated television series, *Hart to Hart.* And Natalie Wood was making *Brainstorm,* an MGM motion picture in which her co-star was Christopher Walken. The Wagners invited Walken to join them on their yacht in Catalina for the holiday weekend.

Bad weather was predicted for the night of November 28. A cold piercing rain swept over Isthmus Bay, pummeling the faces of those going ashore in small boats for dinner. But the sea was not rough, and the dinghies had no difficulty negotiating the waves. Twice, earlier that day, Paul Miller had seen Natalie Wood "buzz" in to shore in her dinghy alone. Then, at about 5 P.M., Miller and three friends eased their own dinghy into a dock and a few minutes later entered the warmth and brightness of Doug's Harbor Reef, where they noticed a party already under way at one table. Natalie Wood, Robert Wagner and Christopher Walken were gaily drinking champagne.

About 7 P.M. the Wagner party was seated for dinner, with which they ordered more champagne. They were still enjoying themselves when Miller and his friends left. But Don Whiting, the night manager of the restaurant, was worried. He felt that the Wagners were so intoxicated they might not make it back to their yacht. When they left the restaurant at 10:30 P.M., he called Kurt Craig of the Harbor Patrol and asked him to make certain the group reached their yacht safely in the dinghy.

Later that night, aboard *Easy Rider,* Miller and his wife couldn't sleep. Their quarters were in the bow of their boat, facing the shore, and in a house on that shore a party was raging. Two loudspeakers had been set up on a porch, and the sound of rock music blaring across the cove was keeping the Millers awake. This may have been the party noise which Marilyn Wayne, who heard Natalie Wood's cries, believed was coming from another boat. At 1:15 A.M. Miller sat up, reached wearily for the radio microphone, and turned to the harbor channel, which all boats monitor. He intended to call the Bay Watch, the private Isthmus Bay Coast Guard detail, to ask them to quiet the party on the beach.

"Bay Watch, this is *Easy Rider.*"

Nothing but crackling static, and Miller realized at once that the man from the Bay Watch must be at the party.

Suddenly the radio sprang to life with a different voice. It was Robert Wagner, although Miller didn't recognize his voice at first. He didn't sound nervous or excited. Miller described Wagner's tone as "quizzical" as he said, *"Easy Rider,* are you cruising in the vicinity?"

"No."

"Well, this is *Splendour.* We think we may have someone missing in an eleven-foot rubber dinghy."

Don Whiting, the night manager of the restaurant, was reading a paperback book in the cabin of the boat on which he lived year round, when the radio beside him crackled and he heard the conversation between Wagner and Miller. Whiting radioed a friend on the isthmus to go to the Wagner yacht at once and report back to him about the situation.

Thirty minutes later, light beams from Harbor Patrol boats, private boats of the Bay Watch, and Coast Guard helicopters began to crisscross the ocean. The beams illuminated rolling waves and swept over yachts and sailing ships rocking in the swells—but nothing was found in the sea.

At seven-thirty the following morning a Sheriff's Office helicopter was heading toward Catalina to aid in the search when suddenly one of the crew members detected a spot of red in the ocean waves below. "Go down," he shouted to the pilot. The helicopter descended toward the sea, the wind from its rotor blades churning the water beneath them. Face down, in a red jacket, Natalie Wood floated, her hair splayed out in the water.

The location of her body was no less than one mile south of the Wagner yacht, off an isolated cove known as Blue Cavern Point. The missing dinghy was discovered on the shore, even farther to the south. The key in the ignition of the boat was turned to the off position, the gear was in neutral, and the oars were tied down.

Police were surprised, because the boat obviously had not been used. Even more startling was Natalie Wood's clothing. She was clad only in a nightgown, knee-length wool socks and a down-filled jacket. It was apparent that she had not dressed for a boat ride —and yet police believed she must have untied the line which held the dinghy to the yacht. But why had she untied it if she didn't intend to go out in the boat? That was only one of the mysteries surrounding her tragic death.

On the day Natalie Wood's body was found, I dispatched Pamela Eaker, a skilled investigator on the Medical Examiner's staff, to Catalina. Eaker interrogated Robert Wagner, who told her that after they had returned from the restaurant that night he and Walken went to the wardroom of the yacht for a nightcap while Natalie retired to her quarters. The last time he remembered seeing his wife was at about quarter of eleven. Then, sometime after midnight, Wagner went to their cabin and noticed that his wife was not in bed. When he searched for her elsewhere on the yacht, he discovered that the dinghy was also missing. Even so, he said, he wasn't concerned at first, because his wife often took the boat out alone. But as time passed and she didn't reappear, he became more and more upset, and finally radioed for help.

Eaker asked Wagner if it was possible that his wife had taken her own life. Wagner said that his wife was definitely not suicidal.

Eaker also spoke to Don Whiting, the restaurant manager, and to various sheriff's deputies and Santa Monica detectives. Her official report described the findings up to that point in the investigation and concluded:

> Decedent's body had been taken from the ocean and placed in the Hyperbaric Chamber for safe-keeping. Upon this investigator's arrival at

location, decedent observed lying in "stokes litter." Decedent is wrapped in plastic sheet, she herself is dressed in flannel nightgown and socks. The jacket that she was wearing when found floating is no longer on the body, having come off when she was pulled from the water. At time decedent was pulled from the water, Sheriff's personnel say that body was absent of any rigor and they noted foam coming from mouth. Decedent still has foam coming from mouth. Rigor is now present of a 3 to 4+ throughout her entire body. Decedent has numerous bruises to legs and arms. Decedent's eyes are also a bit cloudy appearing. No other trauma noted and foul play is not suspected at this time.

Nor did police suspect foul play in Natalie Wood's death, but by nightfall on that Sunday Hollywood was alive with rumors. Wasn't it strange that the two men on the yacht didn't even know that she had left the boat? Hadn't she spoken to them? Why had she slipped out to the stern of the yacht in the middle of the night, climbed down a ladder, and untied the dinghy? What was she doing? Where was she going? And why?

In any case of unusual death, it is the first duty of medical examiners to suspect murder. Indeed, some authorities on forensic science argue that the search for murder is our *only* real mission, and that anything else we accomplish is merely additional service to the community above and beyond that primary duty.

I believe that forensic science is—and should be—broader in its horizons. But I concur with those authorities in one particular: every death is a homicide, until proven otherwise. So, even while Pamela Eaker was interrogating people on the island, I was telephoning Paul Miller, my host on that fact-finding mission three years before. I wanted a special investigation to be conducted by an expert to determine the facts of Natalie Wood's death. And when I learned that Miller had been there at Isthmus Bay that very night, I was convinced his report would be conclusive.

I gave Miller some specific instructions which were basic to any forensic investigation of such a tragedy:

1. Examine the stern of the Wagners' yacht for any disturbance, or evidence of violence, that the police might have missed.

2. Check the dinghy for any sign of a struggle.

3. Examine the algae (marine plant growth) on the bottom of the swimming step for signs of disturbance. (Did she try to reboard the yacht?)

4. Check the sides of the dinghy for fingernail scratches. (Did she try to climb into the dinghy?)

But these questions should be only the beginning, I stressed to Miller. I was relying on his experience and knowledge for the complete investigation.

When I hung up, I was pleased that I had commissioned the right man in the right location for the job. But I also knew that his special report might take days, and the public was demanding to know now what had happened to Natalie Wood. That first morning the whispers were of murder, and I could not deny them. But I hoped that with the information contained in Eaker's fine investigative report, plus the findings of the autopsy to be performed the following day, I would obtain enough data to form a preliminary opinion on the cause of her death, and to replace rumor and speculation with official facts.

That Monday morning, November 30, 1981, was hectic for me. Dr. Sugiyama and Dr. Ishikawa (who was a classmate of mine at Nippon Medical School) were conducting a seminar in forensic science, and I was scheduled to give a breakfast talk to the seminar. But meanwhile the Medical Examiner's Office was besieged by the press, demanding answers to the mystery of Natalie Wood's death. I attended the meeting, said a few words, then apologized for having to leave early.

By nine o'clock the autopsy was ready to begin. It was performed by Dr. Joseph Choi, one of my most skilled deputy medical examiners and Board-certified forensic pathologists. But in supervising the autopsy, I noted some intriguing facts:

A recent diffuse (widespread) bruise, measuring approximately four inches by one inch, spread over the lateral aspect of Natalie Wood's right arm above the wrist. On the left wrist was a slight superficial fresh bruise about a half inch in diameter.

Numerous small superficial skin bruises measuring approximately a half to one inch in diameter were scattered over the right and left lower legs. They appeared to be relatively fresh. The left knee area showed a recent bruise measuring approximately two inches in diameter.

The right ankle had a recent bruise measuring about two inches in diameter, and there were small superficial bruises on the posterior aspect of both lower legs, each measuring a half inch to two inches.

A vertical brush-type abrasion on the left cheek was

the only head wound, and there were no deep traumatic injuries to the skull.

An examination of the clothing Natalie Wood had worn that night revealed other significant facts. More than twenty-four hours after she had been found, the flannel nightgown, the wool socks and the red down jacket were still wet. I picked up the jacket and noted that it was extremely heavy, probably between thirty and forty pounds in its saturated state. I also noted that a report from the toxicology laboratory revealed that the alcohol content of Natalie Wood's blood was .14 percent, .04 percent above the intoxication standard as set by the California Vehicular Code.

From the toxicology report and the bruises we were able to determine the probable cause of death. The vertical abrasion on her cheek told us that Natalie Wood, possibly attempting to board the dinghy, had fallen into the ocean, striking her face. Because she had sustained no deep traumatic head wounds, we knew she had been conscious while in the water. The bruises on her lower legs, I believed at the time, were incurred during her fall.

The saddest part of the story, as far as I was concerned, was revealed in the clothing she had worn. The reason she drowned was the great weight of the jacket, which had pulled her down when she attempted to climb into the dinghy. If she had just taken off that jacket, she might easily have made it into the dinghy, and survived.

The reason she hadn't removed the killing jacket was suggested in the report from the toxicology lab. That .14 percent of alcohol in her blood was, I believed, a deadly factor. She couldn't have been thinking clearly, or she would have slipped off the jacket at once.

On the basis of the autopsy and the other tests we had completed up to that point, I concluded that Natalie Wood had drowned as a result of that wet jacket. I surmised that the untied dinghy, and her body, had drifted a mile away from the yacht on the current. But a question haunted me. When she first fell off the swimming step into the water, why didn't she simply swim a few strokes and reboard the yacht by way of the step? It must have been only a few feet away from her. Even with the heavy jacket, she could have accomplished this effort easily, it seemed to me, for the step, unlike the dinghy, was stable.

Perhaps my investigator on the scene, Eaker, would provide an answer to that mystery. I sent word for her to join me in my office at noon, along with Dr. Ronald Kornblum, the deputy chief of the forensic medicine division, and Dr. Choi, who had performed the autopsy.

My office was on the second floor of Los Angeles County's Forensic Science Center, and we met there as scheduled. The two senior pathologists, Richard Wilson, my administrative chief of staff, and investigator Eaker sat across from me as I outlined my preliminary finding of an accidental drowning, adding that alcohol had played a significant role in Natalie Wood's death. One of my staff said, "What the reporters out there are really interested in, Dr. Noguchi, isn't so much whether Natalie Wood was intoxicated or not, but *why she left the yacht in the middle of the night.*"

I nodded. The question tied in with my own. Why hadn't she climbed back aboard the yacht when she

was only one or two feet away? Both actions seemed
to indicate that she was determined to get away from
the yacht. It was then I was told that one of the sheriff's deputies had apparently reported that Wagner
and Walken were quarreling in the main cabin that
night. In theory, it was possible that Natalie Wood
became disgusted with them and tried to take off in
the dinghy just to get away.

Silence filled the room. All of us were taken aback
by the implications of this idea. It fed right into the
hands of those who had been speculating that some
"scandal" on the yacht had contributed to the famous
star's death.

I've attended many dramatic news conferences
after the deaths of world-famous motion picture stars,
but none so tense as the one following Natalie Wood's
death. Rumors of foul play, as well as of sexual scandal, were rocketing through the movie colony. And it
was my responsibility to produce the facts that would
rebut or substantiate those rumors.

Ironically, an almost identical scene had greeted me
only two weeks before when I announced my findings
concerning the accidental death of another famous
movie actor, William Holden, who had been the intimate friend of Stephanie Powers, Robert Wagner's co-
star in the television series *Hart to Hart*. Now the
reporters listened no less avidly as I stated our preliminary findings on Natalie Wood's death: "She slipped
and drowned accidentally while attempting to enter an
inflatable boat to leave the yacht." I said there was no
evidence of foul play. A scrape on her left cheek was

consistent with her falling and having struck the dinghy as she went into the water.

Then, fully mindful of the William Holden case, I hesitated. I didn't relish another storm of criticism like the one that had been launched against me when I revealed that alcohol had contributed to Holden's death. But now, with almost the same facts in my possession in Natalie Wood's case, I couldn't lie. The toxicological tests had been performed. By law they must be included in the official public record. And every reporter who saw the .14 percent blood-alcohol reading would immediately know that it was well above the .10 percent alcoholic level which is defined as legal intoxication by the California Vehicular Code.

Nevertheless, I tried to soft-pedal the information. I said there had been only "recreational" drinking going on that Saturday evening when the Wagners went ashore on Catalina Island for dinner. "I don't believe drunkenness caused her to fall into the water in the first place," I continued. "The point one four level of alcohol in the blood means she was only 'slightly intoxicated.' She apparently was having wine, champagne—perhaps seven or eight glasses. That would certainly not cause a person to be drunk."

What I said was true, but I was purposely modifying the facts. I didn't remind the reporters of one significant forensic detail. The alcohol level, of course, had actually been *higher* than .14 percent at the time Natalie Wood fell into the water.

A reporter asked, "Did intoxication play *any* role in her death?"

I thought of the soaked jacket that could have been shrugged off and said, "The intoxication was one of the factors involved in the fact that she was not able to respond well to the emergency, after she was in the water.''

Thus I toned down the toxicological evidence as best I could, while still telling the truth. But then the questioning turned to an even more controversial area. I believe it was the NBC television reporter who inquired why Natalie Wood left the yacht in the first place.

I said I didn't know and suggested we might learn through a "psychological autopsy" why she felt she should separate herself from her husband and Walken that night.

No luck. The bombshell question exploded, showing that the press already *knew*. "Dr. Noguchi, was there a dispute on that yacht between Robert Wagner and Christopher Walken that caused Natalie Wood to leave?"

I held up my hand. "Just a moment," I said and turned to Richard Wilson, whom I had asked to attend the conference. He was in charge of press liaison and had received information about the argument. So, as the reporters watched, I called him to my side. I was seated behind a microphone as he knelt beside me, and I don't think he was aware that he could be heard over the microphone. "Yes," he told me, "there *was* an argument.''

I turned to the press, knowing they had already heard Wilson's statement, but repeated it for the record.

"What kind of an argument?" one reporter shouted.

I nodded to Wilson, who said, in a lower voice, "Nonviolent.''

I said, "It was a nonviolent argument."

By then the room was in an uproar. The dispute was big news. An argument, nonviolent or not, could mean that Wagner had indirectly contributed to his wife's death. That would be front-page copy. And it was only the beginning. The quarrel might open the door to further speculations of a sensational nature about what had actually taken place among these three "beautiful people" on that yacht.

By now the reporters knew that Richard Wilson was the man with the information, and they battered him with questions. But Wilson said he didn't know what the dispute was about, only that it was a heated conversation on a variety of subjects. In response to another question, he replied that the dispute was not over Natalie Wood.

"They were arguing for general purposes," Wilson said. "We don't know exactly why. There was no physical altercation. Each of the two gentlemen was examined."

Still the questions came. "Did she try to leave the yacht because she believed she was physically endangered?"

"According to the information we have, no," Wilson said. "She felt no danger at all. The argument was not over her."

As the reporters hammered away at Wilson, I grew more and more uneasy. The question of the quarrel had bothered me before the press conference, and now it bothered me even more.

The reasons for my unease were twofold. One, the information was thirdhand, as far as I was concerned. A deputy sheriff had apparently told a staff member, who informed me, that there had been an argument. And secondly, there was the consideration that always bedevils all medical examiners: how much information should be revealed if it is not directly relevant?

In this case, a shouting match between Wagner and Walken which caused Natalie Wood to leave the yacht, even if true, was a peripheral matter as far as I was concerned. But the law charges medical examiners with discovery of "the manner, cause, and circumstance of death"—and such an argument could be construed as a part of the "circumstance."

Still, the dispute, true or not, was, I believed, a fringe circumstance. It might provide a reason *why* Natalie Wood wanted to take a lonely boat ride that night. But the actual reason for her death was her accidental slip. In more familiar terms, it's as if a husband and wife engage in a verbal fight, and the wife angrily runs out of the house, drives away in a car, and is killed in a crash because she accidentally steps on the accelerator instead of the brake. The husband is not guilty of murder.

But the press was hot on the Wagner trail, determined to discover what had really transpired on that yacht during the night which caused Natalie Wood to leave in such a hurry that she didn't even dress. And they had already picked up the scent from other sources. Sergeant Sue Maher of the Sheriff's Information Bureau told a Los Angeles *Times* reporter that "investigators confirmed that there was some kind of interaction between Wagner and Walken—but we don't know whether it was heated or whether they were just joking around."

The next day friends of Robert Wagner, who had

been in seclusion ever since the accident, sought to still the rumors. They circulated word to reporters that there had been no dispute at all on the yacht. Instead, they said, Natalie Wood had been unable to sleep because the dinghy was knocking against the stern of the yacht. She had gone topside to adjust the line to the dinghy, had slipped while doing so, and fallen into the water.

I found that theory plausible, particularly because it explained her nightgown-and-socks apparel. And yet there was a possible flaw. The dinghy was rubber, and, according to Paul Miller, our expert who owned a similar boat, a rubber dinghy makes little or no noise when it strikes a yacht. Silence is relative, however, and other sailors say that the noise might be amplified to an annoying degree when you are on the inside of the boat.

I called Miller. "What have you found so far?" I asked.

"To begin with, I've made a preliminary investigation of the yacht and the dinghy, and I've got the answers to your basic questions."

I listened attentively.

"No murder," he said. "There weren't any signs of a struggle in the yacht or the dinghy. There *were* fingernail scratches on the starboard side of the dinghy, which shows she was trying to climb into it."

"And the swimming step on the yacht?"

"The algae was untouched. She never tried to reboard the yacht."

While I was thinking that over, he said, "But that isn't the interesting part. It's how she died."

"What do you mean?"

"Everyone, including you and Robert Wagner, seems to agree on one thing: that she fell into the water next to the yacht and drowned. No way."

"What do you mean?"

"The dinghy would never have been found where it was, on the beach a mile from the bay. There's no way it could have gotten there *unless Natalie Wood took it there.*"

Silence. Then I said, "You mean she rode the dinghy there and *then* fell out?"

"Look, it's more complicated than that. I'll put the report together with all the facts and then you'll understand."

After I hung up the phone, I was intrigued by the possibilities of Miller's investigation. But at the same time I was concerned with a new problem. The investigation was obviously turning up new facts—and I was already under attack for releasing too many details at yesterday's news conference. In fact, the press had reported the conference in such a way that I, not Wilson, appeared to have revealed to the reporters the information from police about the shipboard quarrel. As the Los Angeles *Times* said, "Interviews with those present, Noguchi said, produced the information that upon the party's return to the yacht . . . Wagner and Walken engaged in a 'non-violent argument.' "

Hollywood was, of course, steaming with the news. And it seemed, from reports of the rumors that reached me, that many of the movie colony disbelieved Wagner—and actually thought that much more than an "argument" had taken place that night on the yacht. Scandalous stories and weird sexual allegations were spreading like brushfire.

Thirteen years as Chief Medical Examiner of a county which included Hollywood had given me ample experience with that sort of rumor—beginning as far back as Marilyn Monroe. Because many people believe that Hollywood is a sin capital where glamorous people with too much money are constantly searching for new kicks, they are always eager to believe the worst. And a generation of sensationalist tabloids such as the *Enquirer*, the *Globe* and the *Star* has fattened with profits on this mind-set of the public.

There may be a kernel of truth in this view of Hollywood, which the tabloids expand to grotesque dimensions. As a medical examiner, I have investigated all kinds of bizarre sex-related deaths, from sadistic to autoerotic to "kinky." My professional experience had been wide. Yet in this case I believed Robert Wagner. He and Natalie Wood had been married for years. The very evening of the tragedy they had enjoyed a happy dinner at Doug's Harbor Reef, complete with champagne. The evidence seemed to preclude any scandalous behavior. Yet any wife can become annoyed with her husband at times, and, according to reports, when Natalie Wood was upset she would in fact rush out alone to "get away from it all."

The controversy grew even more heated when those in Hollywood who believed Wagner flew to his defense—and I became the main target. On Wednesday of that week, for example, the *Times* front-page story was headlined DISPUTE BEFORE WOOD'S DEATH NOW IN DOUBT. Its opening paragraphs read:

A Sheriff's homicide detective Tuesday disputed coroner's statements suggesting that Robert Wagner and Christopher Walken were arguing heatedly aboard an anchored yacht when Wagner's wife, actress Natalie Wood, drowned.

"I don't know where the coroner got that information," said investigator Roy Hamilton. "We talked to Wagner and Walken and there was no indication that there was any kind of an argument."

But it was the next quote from Hamilton which hurt the most. He said, according to the *Times,* "I think he (Los Angeles County Coroner Thomas T. Noguchi) was juicing it up a little bit."

I was no stranger to such slurs. In 1969 I had been on the receiving end of much worse insults when the County Board of Supervisors sought to fire me. But the charges brought against me were so laughable that Los Angeles citizens had rallied to my support and every charge was ruled "disproved." I remained in my post, and the next twelve years had seen forensic science prosper in Los Angeles. A new Forensic Science Center had been built under my supervision, and Los Angeles was now generally considered a focal point of modern forensic research. A month earlier, medical examiners around the country had made me the president-elect of their national association.

And then William Holden had died, and I told the truth. His alcoholic level was a factor in his death. But Holden's friends protested angrily that I should not have revealed his intoxication. And now, only two weeks later, Natalie Wood had perished in tragic circumstances, and I not only reported on alcohol intoxication again but was also accused of "juicing it up a little bit" in a report of the argument which had come not from my department but from the police.

Thus the controversy surrounding the circumstances of Natalie Wood's death now grew to include controversy about me. Some Hollywood stars, still fretting over the William Holden report, struck hard at me, as well as at the *Times* for printing the remarks of the "stage-struck" coroner. Frank Sinatra sent a letter to the Board of Supervisors which said, in effect, that coroners should be seen and not heard. And the Screen Actors Guild dispatched its own wire lambasting me for invasion of privacy.

When Paul Miller's report on the real facts of the death of Natalie Wood arrived, I read it—and decided not to release the document to the press. It added details the media would only call "gory" and "sensational." The report did not alter the official coroner's conclusion of an accidental drowning. So, rather than create more media indignation over "too many details," I reluctantly filed away that report. This is the first time the facts it uncovered, which re-create Natalie Wood's last moments, have been revealed by me. And it is both a tragic and a heroic story.

Rereading the report today, I can see Isthmus Bay again in my mind's eye, dark and threatening in the night, the cold rain slanting down upon ships rocking in the water. And I recall the day Miller brought me the report. We sat in my apartment in Marina Del Rey, overlooking the same ocean which broke against the shores of Santa Catalina thirty miles to the west.

Miller leaned toward me earnestly as he said, "You had it wrong, Tom. Natalie Wood didn't die like you think. She had class."

He drew a map of Isthmus Bay showing where the boats, including *Splendour,* were moored that night. Then he drew an arrow from the west, passing through the island mountains and pointing toward the ships in the bay. "The basic factor is the wind funnel," he said.

From my own observations of the island on my trip three years before, I knew the phenomenon to which he referred. The jet stream sweeps from the west over Catalina Island, and in the mountains it forms a funnel which blows straight down into the bay where the Wagners' yacht was moored. *Splendour* faced into the wind, as did its dinghy tied to the stern.

"After she untied the line," Miller continued, "the dinghy would have been blown out toward the mainland. It would never have made a ninety-degree turn and headed down the coast with the wind funnel hitting it from the side. Remember, an inflatable boat in the water is like a balloon with the wind blowing it."

It was cold that night when Natalie Wood, dressed only in a nightgown, wool socks and a down jacket, appeared on the deck of *Splendour* and descended the swimming step to the dinghy. Was she angry at her husband and rushing off alone? Forensic evidence, such as the fingernail scratches on the side of the dinghy, the brush-type abrasion on her cheek, and the untouched algae on the swim step, seemed to indicate that she was trying to board the dinghy, not just adjust its rope, when the accident happened.

But Miller's evidence provided the possibility of a third explanation, which, according to my interpretation, confirmed Wagner's story of the accident. Considering the wind funnel, when Natalie Wood, for whatever reason, untied the boat, the wind was strong and would have pushed it away from the yacht. And it is quite possible that, instead of trying to step into the dinghy, she might have been reaching for it and lost her balance.

Whatever her purpose, she fell—and the cold water closed over her head. But when she bobbed to the surface, she must have felt there was no danger. She was still only a few feet away from the safety of the yacht. Not only that, she had taken hold of the inflatable boat. The widespread bruise on her right arm showed that she hooked her arm over the side of the dinghy, knowing the boat would hold her up safely until she caught her breath.

Too late, she must have realized something strange was happening. She and the dinghy were being swept swiftly away from the yacht—ten yards, twenty, thirty. She hadn't realized the strength of the wind funnel. Within seconds the dinghy was moving farther and farther out in the water, too distant for her to swim back to the yacht.

She must have called out for help at that point. But her cries went unheard on *Splendour,* and on other vessels too. The rock music blaring from loudspeakers at the party ashore drowned out Natalie Wood's desperate calls from the surface of the dark sea. Yet there was still hope. Miss Wayne and her friend *did* hear her shouts. But when they looked outside, they could see nothing in the dark, and they thought they heard people on a neighboring boat say they were coming to her rescue.

Now Natalie Wood was no doubt becoming really frightened. Her cries were going unheard. No lights played across the water, no boats started out to her rescue. Still, she felt she was safe because of the dinghy. She could crawl into it, start its engine, and be back to the warmth of the yacht in minutes.

But it was then that she must have suffered her most terrifying shock. She tried to climb aboard the dinghy which would save her, and discovered she couldn't do it. The rubber sides of the dinghy were large and cylindrical; it would have been difficult in the best of circumstances for her to reach over them from the water to hoist herself up. Forensic evidence revealed that she may have gone to the rear of the boat and used the motor for leverage. There was a metal frame beneath the motor in which you can place your foot. Swimmers often use this technique: with your back to the dinghy, you place one arm around the motor and a foot in the brace, and push up to board the dinghy from the water. The bruises on the back of Natalie Wood's lower legs suggested she may have tried to do that.

But it didn't work. She couldn't make it into the boat. Frantically, she attempted again and again to hoist her body up into the safety of the dinghy—but the jacket dragged her back down into the water every time.

Finally she realized she was being swept into mortal danger as the dinghy pulled her farther and farther out toward the open sea. She might drown or die of hypothermia, the loss of body temperature, in the icy water. What could she do?

Natalie Wood fought for her life in that cold November ocean. She did not give up. Instead, she began to perform a feat that was both unique and gallant. And she almost achieved a miracle.

Clinging to a boat being swept out into the open sea, her body already becoming numb in the cold water, she decided that her only hope was somehow to propel that dinghy into the teeth of the wind, back toward the shore of Catalina. It must have seemed hopeless at first. The wind pushed the boat like an air bubble. But, desperately, she started kicking her legs as hard as she could, and paddling the water with her free arm.

And it worked. The boat ceased its movement out to sea and started, ever so slowly, back toward the island—and safety.

A mild current of one knot was running south, and, paddling in a dark, windy sea beside the dinghy, she pushed the boat along with the current, edging it ever closer toward the shore. But the southern drift took her away from the safe harbor with its yachts whose lights shone in the distance. In fact, the bay was now behind her. But she was approaching closer and closer to the beach—four hundred yards, three hundred fifty yards. If she could just hang on, she would be safe on the shore.

But numbness now crept all through her body. The heavy jacket pulled her down, and its weight sapped her strength. Fighting in the ocean, she saw the cove ahead. Blue Cavern Point. No boats lay at anchor there, but it was a haven from the wind which was her enemy. Minutes to go. She must keep paddling.

Natalie Wood, a brave young woman, tragically lost her fight against the specter, death, less than two hundred yards from shore. Hypothermia caused her to lose strength, then consciousness, then finally her last feeble grip on the boat. She sank beneath the waves and drowned.

Only minutes later, the boat she had so painfully and courageously maneuvered for a mile landed safely on the beach.

2

Getting
Started

Even as the controversy surrounding Natalie Wood's death subsided, the attacks on me for "exploiting" both her death and William Holden's multiplied, and suddenly I knew I was facing the deepest crisis in my professional life. Criticism came not only from the Hollywood community concerned about the privacy issue, but also from public officials who were disturbed about the way I was performing my job. Was I a "ham," "juicing it up" for "personal publicity," as some said, or a medical examiner fighting for a principle?

My career of twenty-one years' service would teeter on the brink when that issue was finally adjudicated. But I'll admit there were times in the early days of my legal struggle when I began to wonder if I had made a mistake by leaving the home of my ancestors, Japan.

And at moments like that I always took courage from my memories of my father.

Wataru Noguchi came from a farming family on the little western island of Shikoku. In those days in Japan, the influence of the caste system was still strong, even though the shogun era had ended in the 1860s. If you were born a farmer, you remained a farmer. If you were born a samurai warrior, you stayed a samurai. (The grandfather of my mother, Tomika Narahashi, was a samurai, the chief swordsman to the regional lord of Oita, a district of Kyushu Island.) There was no way to break out of your heritage, no matter what it was.

Yet my father did it. He simply decided he wanted to be an artist, not a man tilling the soil. His family and neighbors were aghast when he abandoned the farm of his ancestors and departed for Tokyo. As the oldest son, he would have inherited the land. Instead, in 1910 he gave it all up to his relatives and left for a life of art, becoming a painter in the Impressionist tradition.

Not that my father was ever "bohemian," as artists in those days were sometimes described. Far from it. My relationship to him, as a child, was always formal in the Japanese tradition. For example, if I wanted to talk to him, I would say, "Honorable father, may I speak?" "Yes, you may," he would reply. But my father was, in his way, a completely free spirit, incredible in Japan in that era.

One day a little boy came to him crying. There was dirt in his eye, and my father struggled to help, but could do nothing to relieve his misery. Finally he escorted the boy to a doctor, who simply placed a small drop of medicine in the child's eye and cured the pain.

At that moment, my father saw a new path of knowledge. Raised as a farmer, he had broken the mold to become an artist. Now he saw the wonder of healing and desired to know more about it. So, at the late age of thirty-three, he decided to enter medical school. He was forty years old by the time he became a doctor. But the age problem didn't faze him any more than the caste tradition had done years before. He was invited to be the chief of the eye, ear, nose and throat department in a hospital in Yokosuka, and in 1940 he opened his private practice in that city.

I was then thirteen years old. All through my school years I had strained my teachers' patience with my love of mischief, but I received good grades and because I idolized my father I decided that I too would become a physician. Another factor entered into that decision. My younger brother Kazuo suffered from birth from cerebral palsy. For years I carried my crippled brother three miles back and forth to school, strapped to a bicycle I had specially rigged. And I helped him get around in school because he couldn't move unaided. If I became a doctor, I thought, I might be able to find a cure for that mysterious disease. But then when I was thirteen another event occurred that would have a lasting effect on me and play a role in my ultimate choice of career.

My father had asked me to bring something from home to his office. He was treating a young man when I arrived, and I sat down in the outer room and waited for him to finish. Suddenly a buzzer startled me. The nurse at the reception desk jumped when she heard my father call her. And I could hear terrible sounds of gasping as I ran pell-mell after her into my father's office. There I saw him kneeling beside his patient, who was on the floor, and giving him mouth-to-mouth resuscitation. Then he stopped. I came closer and observed the young man lying perfectly still. It was the first dead body I had ever seen.

Later I discovered what had happened. The patient was suffering from a strep throat and my father had swabbed it with Lugol solution, which contains iodine —the standard practice at the time. But the young man had begun to gasp and had fallen to the floor. Almost at once, he had gone into an irreversible coma.

What followed was to be the most harrowing period of my father's life, for the parents of the young man immediately accused him of medical malpractice, claiming their son had choked to death on the cotton swab my father had used to apply the iodine solution. The district attorney's office took up the case, and my father was charged with carelessly using loose cotton and thus causing his patient to choke and die. Under the Japanese Penal Code, he could be sent to prison if convicted.

One can imagine the turmoil and despair in our family. My father, so upright all his life, faced disgrace and imprisonment. It seemed to us that the DA's office had already convicted him without a shred of evidence.

Japan, like the United States in the 1930s, was backward in forensic medicine. Only in very rare cases was an autopsy performed, and that occurred almost always at the request of the family of the decedent. There were no coroners' or medical examiners' offices in Japan then. That's why my father created a sensation when he demanded an autopsy even though the young man's parents had requested none. He told the authorities he would accept the results of such an autopsy, even if it meant prison.

The autopsy was performed by one of Yokosuka's most distinguished physicians. And the examination of the young man's throat and lungs showed not one trace of cotton from the swab. In fact, the autopsy determined that the man had died of an allergic reaction to iodine, with no previous history of such an allergy. My father was cleared. And a thirteen-year-old boy received a first—and enduring—impression of the role of forensic medicine.

I learned another important lesson during the closing months of the war with America. In March of 1945 I was eighteen, a sophomore in college, when the sound of air raid sirens split the air over Tokyo. Then the distant chatter of antiaircraft guns was heard, and our professor quickly ran to the door, gesturing for us to follow.

Sitting in that classroom, I could look up directly into the sky, for the roof had been blown off the school building in a previous raid. Since then our classes had convened in the rubble, where the students, as well as the professor, wore helmets and shoulder pads. The professor lectured and we took notes until, almost every day, the air raid sirens sounded.

That day I followed after the professor, who was running toward the trenches we had dug for shelter around the perimeter of the school grounds. And as thunderous explosions struck closer and closer, I jumped into a trench along with the august professor himself. I've never forgotten that man, because of his courage and composure. In the middle of the detonations, he sat against the dirt wall of the trench and proceeded to mark examination papers as calmly as if he were in his study at home.

The war ended with the horrifying destruction of Hiroshima and Nagasaki by nuclear bombs. And then we were "invaded" by the American army of occupation. Japanese propaganda films during the war had depicted Americans as "apes" and "monsters," but the ones I met were friendly, open and often laughing —a strange warrior tribe indeed. I discovered that I liked these laughing people who somehow possessed so much scientific greatness that they had easily overpowered Japan, with all her brave soldiers.

After the war, still determined to become a doctor, I enrolled in Nippon Medical School. But remembering what had happened to my father, I knew that I wanted to learn law as well as medicine. So I took an almost unprecedented step: the year after I enrolled in medical school in 1947, I also enrolled in law school. It was a hectic time, studying medicine during the day and law at night. I wonder now how I was able to do it. In 1951 I graduated from Nippon Medical School and interned at Tokyo University Hospital. But all the while a new dream was forming in my mind. I wanted to go to America.

Why did I decide to effect that startling transformation in my future life? I could have inherited my father's substantial practice and become a wealthy physician in Japan. But it was not his success that inspired my decision. Rather it was my subconscious desire to superachieve as my father had done. He had broken through barriers when he left the family to become first an artist, then a doctor. I wanted to break new ground myself. And, from the first, I had been fascinated with the wonders of science—and there was no doubt that the United States, in 1952, was the world leader in technology.

My parents were startled, and I'm sure my father was distressed that I would not carry on the practice he had spent so many years developing. But once my mind was made up, they made no attempt to dissuade me. Discouragement came from another quarter when I applied to two hundred American hospitals for an internship. My record showed excellent grades, and yet I received only one reply—from Orange County General Hospital, in California. They accepted me, and in 1952 I flew to this great country, America, for the first time.

I have never really regretted my decision to make America my home, even though I quickly found that the U.S. government had not been just to its Japanese-American citizens during the war. One of those citizens, a pretty girl named Hisako Nishihara, was a freshman at the University of California at Los Angeles when she and her family were uprooted from their home in Los Angeles and placed in detention camps, where they remained throughout the war.

Hisako and I fell in love and were married on December 31, 1960. At that time I was studying clinical and anatomic pathology, because I had discovered another instinct within myself: a love for scientific detective work, which is an integral part of a pathologist's profession. Normally I would have elected to pursue a private practice in pathology. But since my father's brush with legal disaster my sights were set on another goal: the practice of forensic medicine.

The trouble was, as my peers quickly warned me, there was no money in it. Most practitioners in forensic medicine were in government service, and I would have to resign myself to a lifetime of low income if I opted for that as a career. Yet it was the very fact that forensic medicine was held in such low regard that attracted me to it. Here was a field in which one man could make a difference. In fact, it desperately needed good men to elevate its standards and fulfill its mission.

So I applied to the Los Angeles coroner's office in 1960 and went to work there as a deputy medical examiner. Despite the drab quarters and the low pay, I quickly realized I had made the proper choice. For I was fascinated with forensic medicine, perhaps the most colorful of the medical disciplines, with a picturesque history that harked back to the days of Robin Hood.

Forensic medicine came into being with a crime that shook Europe in 1192, and because of that crime a new title was established for certain knights of the English realm: coroner.

King Richard the Lion-Hearted, on his way home from the Crusades, was kidnapped by Leopold of Austria, and an enormous ransom was demanded from England for his return. But the King's treasury wasn't large enough to pay the ransom. And it seemed that Richard, lion heart and all, was doomed.

In that crisis, the savior was not the legendary Robin Hood, as folk tradition has it, but a man more prosaically named Hubert Walter, the Justiciar of England. Desperately, Walter searched for ways to raise the ransom money—and came up with a novel source: corpses. In those days almost all convicted felons were hanged or otherwise disposed of in an unpleasant manner. Walter appointed a knight in each shire to take custody of felons' property for the royal treasury, and gave him the title "coroner," derived from the Latin *custos placitorum coronae,* "guardian of the pleas [claims] of the crown." Sometimes the coroner even sold the death weapon, if it had value. But another method by which coroners raised money from the dead was more important to medical historians, because, in effect, it began the profession of forensic medicine as it is known today.

England was a mixture of Norman and Saxon citizenry. The Saxons were English, but the invading Normans were the ruling class. It was perfectly legal for a Norman to murder a Saxon, as far as the rulers were concerned. But if you killed a Norman, you were in trouble. In fact, you had to produce the killer or *prove* that the dead man was not a Norman or the entire village would be required to pay a heavy fine. The fine was called a "murdrum." And to determine if it could be levied, coroners held inquests into the facts of every suspicious death, investigations which were the genesis of our profession today. Over the years, other agencies gradually assumed the tasks of levying and collecting taxes, but the coroner's function of investigating mysterious deaths remained.

The growth of forensic medicine as a medical discipline occurred on the European Continent, where, in 1621, the "Father of Legal Medicine," Paulo Zacchias, who had been appointed the Pope's physician in the Vatican, published a textbook entitled *Questiones medico legales* which analyzed various medically related cases heard by the papal court. His book became the standard text in its field for centuries. But still in England forensic medicine was not accepted by the medical establishment. Instead, laymen were appointed as coroners and they performed bureaucratic duties, not medical.

This system of laymen coroners traveled to the new continent called America. In fact, for hundreds of years in this country the only qualification to run for the office of coroner was that you had no prison record. But America kept growing. Cities of ten thousand became metropolitan areas of millions, and the unexplained deaths, homicides, suicides and accidents multiplied rapidly. Finally, in 1912, Massachusetts became the first state in the Union to pass a statute establishing a medical examiner's system, with physicians, not laymen, as coroners.

Gradually the same laws were promulgated in almost all states of the Union, including California in 1956. By then, forensic science had come a long way from the time of Norman rule and from theories in the mind of a Vatican physician. Modern forensic science can be defined as the scientific investigation of the cause of death in unexplained circumstances, particularly when criminal activity is suspected. And today the field has grown to encompass several areas of expertise.

Forensic pathologists determine the cause of death by directing the examination of the body, its tissues and biological fluids. Under the forensic pathologist's supervision, other experts engage in various disciplines:

1. Criminalistics, the branch of science which deals with trace evidence such as paint chips, soil, hair, clothing, as well as firearms and other weapons.

2. Toxicology, which deals with determination and interpretation of poisons, drugs and toxic chemicals found in the tissues, blood and other biological fluids.

3. Histology, which studies structural changes in human tissue caused by disease or violence.

4. Forensic dentistry and anthropology, which assist in the identification of bodies through teeth or skeletal remains.

Those are the major disciplines which come under the purview of the modern medical examiner. In addition, in some medical examiners' offices, there are experts in forensic psychiatry, forensic microscopy, questioned-document examination, forensic engineering, medical jurisprudence and other forensic disciplines.

Nowadays medical-examiner offices in large urban areas include numerous departments with skilled investigators and/or medical examiners who visit the scene of the crime and search for forensic clues, and a staff of forensic pathologists who perform the autopsies to obtain and interpret medical evidence and conduct a medicolegal investigation, coordinating with toxicologists, histologists and other technicians who examine and analyze samples of tissue and fluid, searching for clues.

Thus we attack each unexplained death from many scientific directions, with skilled experts and laboratory equipment. And we can learn—and educate everyone—about dangers ranging from the existence of poisoned Tylenol capsules to the identity of a murderer who may think he has committed the "perfect crime." But when I joined the Los Angeles Medical Examiner's staff, we did not have this large modern organization. Instead, the office employed only three full-time pathologists, a handful of laboratory technicians and some young part-time residents studying to be pathologists.

And into this small complex came the most famous decedent in the world.

3

Medical Examiner's Case No. 81128

Marilyn
Monroe

It was incredible. On November 4, 1982, I was on my way by car to the Los Angeles District Attorney's Office to be interviewed about a possible murder. The unbelievable factor was that the "murder" had occurred no less than twenty years earlier. But here in Los Angeles they were still officially investigating the questions which surrounded Marilyn Monroe's death two decades before.

On that date in 1982 I was no longer the Chief Medical Examiner of Los Angeles, because I had been demoted and was in the midst of my appeal to be reinstated. But still the DA wanted to see me. For I was the pathologist who had performed the autopsy on Marilyn Monroe, and, as it happened, the facts revealed in my autopsy report had become the basis for all of the claims of murder. My autopsy, private investigators said, *proved* that Marilyn Monroe was the victim of foul play, even though Theodore J. Curphey, M.D., the Chief Medical Examiner/Coroner in 1962, had concluded on the basis of that same autopsy, plus other evidence, that Marilyn Monroe died from an overdose of Nembutal and chloral hydrate pills. Never in my experience had a coroner's conclusion been so hotly disputed for so long a time.

Over a period of twenty years, I had been questioned by investigative reporters so many times that I had lost count. Many of them were convinced that Senator Robert F. Kennedy was Monroe's lover and had ordered her to be murdered—by injection. They cited evidence of an official cover-up and claimed that a diary Monroe kept had mysteriously disappeared. Finally, public pressure had grown so great that the Los Angeles County District Attorney's Office had been forced to reopen the case, and I was summoned to the Criminal Courts Building and found myself sitting in an office across the desk from two assistant district attorneys. Their questions went right to the points that had bothered investigators for years, beginning with "If Marilyn Monroe swallowed dozens of sleeping pills, why was there no evidence of pills in her digestive tract?"

As I answered that question my mind wandered back to 1962 when I, a young and impressionable medical examiner, first viewed the body of Marilyn Monroe. Later I would be asked, "How did she appear in death?" And I could reply only with words from the Latin poet Petrarch:

It's folly to shrink in fear, if this is dying,

> For death looked lovely in her lovely
> face.

The assistant DAs brought me back to the present with another question: "It's said that the yellow dye on the Nembutal she swallowed should have stained her stomach. And yet you found no evidence of staining. How can that be?"

Again I answered the question, but in the back of my mind I wondered what was there about this beautiful actress that caused such fascination with her life, and such mourning over her death. Why, so many years later, does she still tug on American heartstrings? Her beauty? Her vulnerability? Her talent?

Or the strange unresolved mystery of her relationship with the glamorous Kennedys?

Balloons floated to the ceiling of huge Madison Square Garden. Bands played, elephants trumpeted; the handsome young President of the United States and his dazzling wife looked down on the scene of celebration from a box. It was May 29, 1962, Kennedy's forty-fifth birthday. But the focus of the evening was not the young President. The hundreds of guests eagerly awaited the appearance of the real star of the celebration, perhaps the most talked-about phenomenon in modern motion picture history, the luminous actress Marilyn Monroe.

Earlier that year, President Kennedy had met Monroe in Las Vegas, Nevada, through their mutual friend Frank Sinatra. She had happily agreed to appear at his birthday party and to sing a song for the President. But all the guests knew—as did almost all Americans

—that Marilyn Monroe was perpetually, even rudely, late. Would she keep the President of the United States waiting? Would she embarrass him?

Then suddenly a "pin" light hit a corner of the arena, and Marilyn Monroe entered on an elephant, riding sidesaddle. Dressed in a form-fitting sequin-studded gown, she made her way to a microphone on a platform in the middle of the huge arena, and the audience roared as she began singing in her inimitable baby voice, with heavy sensuous breathing on every syllable:

> "Happy . . . birthday . . . to you
> Happy birthday to . . . you
> Happy birthday . . . dear Mr. President
> Happy birthday to yoooou!"

The tumultuous applause that followed was the climax of the President's birthday party. But, for Monroe, the real summit of the evening may have been reached later at a private party hosted by a Democratic financial supporter, Arthur Krim of United Artists. For there she met Robert F. Kennedy, the President's brother, for the first time.

Adlai Stevenson described the scene at that party in a letter he wrote to Mary Lasker:

Let me tell you about my perilous encounters last night with Marilyn Monroe. She was dressed in what she calls "skin and beads." I didn't see the beads! My encounters, however, were only after breaking through the strong defenses established by Robert Kennedy, who was dodging around her like a moth around the flame.

Also present and hovering, as it happened, was the historian Arthur Schlesinger, who wrote in his diary:

I do not think that I have seen anyone so beautiful; I was enchanted by her manner and her wit, at once so masked, so ingenuous and so penetrating. But one felt a terrible unreality about her—as if talking to someone under water. Bobby and I engaged in mock competition for her; she was most agreeable to him and pleasant to me—but then she receded into her own glittering mist.

That sounded innocent enough, but in his prize-winning biography *Robert Kennedy—And His Times* Schlesinger proceeded to say more, and helped fuel the rumors which have ever since haunted the enigma of Marilyn Monroe's death. "There was something at once magical and desperate about her," Schlesinger wrote.

Robert Kennedy, with his curiosity, his sympathy, his absolute directness of response to distress, in some way got through the glittering mist as few did. He met her again at Patricia Lawford's house in Los Angeles. She called him thereafter in Washington, using an assumed name. She was very often distraught. Angie Novello [a Justice Department aide] talked to her more often than the Attorney General did. One feels that Robert Kennedy came to inhabit the fantasies of her last summer. She dreamily told her friend W. J. Weatherly of the *Manchester Guardian* that she might get married again; someone in politics in Washington; no name vouchsafed. Another friend, Robert Slatzer, claims she said Robert Kennedy had promised to marry her. As Weatherly commented, "Could she possibly believe that Kennedy would ruin himself politically for her?"

Which happens to be exactly the motive a generation of investigative journalists have ascribed as the cause of Marilyn Monroe's death.

Among the most vocal of these journalists was Robert Slatzer, who claimed to have married Monroe briefly in the early fifties and said he remained her lifelong friend. In his book *The Life and Curious Death of Marilyn Monroe,* published in 1974, Slatzer alleged that when Robert Kennedy reneged on his "promise" to marry Monroe she was in a position to blackmail him with her "diary," which mysteriously disappeared after her death. Lending credence to that argument, Los Angeles private investigator Robert Speriglio said he had investigated Slatzer's background and believed he had indeed married Monroe as he said he had. Based on his own investigation, Speriglio also believed Monroe was murdered because of the diary.

In the twenty years since her death, speculations and theories about how and why Marilyn Monroe died have grown as numerous as the theories surrounding the assassinations of President Kennedy and of Robert Kennedy himself. The most prevalent of them called

Monroe's death murder, done to silence her and prevent her from destroying Robert Kennedy's political career. I called her death suicide—both twenty years ago and today—but I admit there are many disturbing questions that have remained unanswered.

Norma Jean Baker was born in Los Angeles General Hospital (now the Los Angeles County–University of Southern California Medical Center), to a mother with a history of mental illness and a "biker" father who deserted her mother before Norma Jean was born and who died in a fiery motorcycle accident not three years later. When her mother was committed to a mental institution, the little girl was sent to live with different sets of foster parents, ranging from whisky-drinking low-lifes to religious fanatics. In between she spent years in a Los Angeles orphanage.

The war saved her. In 1942 women were being hired to work in defense plants, and Norma Jean broke out of her foster-parent straitjacket by acquiring a job at an aircraft factory, where she met and soon married James Dougherty, who represented even more long-range security. But in that same year she was also perceived as an emerging beauty, with soft blond hair, wide, dreamy blue-gray eyes, and a voluptuous figure that drew whistles at the aircraft plant. At war's end she was nineteen, and photographers were asking to snap her picture.

And she still clung to a childhood dream—remembered in a poignant interview a few years later when she was just starting out as a motion picture actress doing bit parts. In an interview with Associated Press columnist James Bacon at the RKO studio, she recalled that she had lived in a foster home near the studio when she was a little girl. She received an allowance of five cents a month from her foster parents, in exchange for which she washed all of the dishes. "They had kids of their own and when Christmas came there was a big tree and all the kids in the house got presents but me. One of the other kids gave me an orange."

Marilyn said she could still remember eating that orange all by herself. "And I could look up and see the RKO studio water tower. I think that's when I decided that someday I would be an actress, and someday I would get inside that studio.

"And here I am," she told Bacon. "It's a real dream come true."

Driven by that dream, Norma Jean divorced Dougherty in 1946 and became one of the countless young girls who arrive in Hollywood each year, knowing that beyond the locked gates of motion picture studios incredible fame and riches can be won—not only by talent, but by a "look," a shape, an inflection of the voice. But success did not come overnight for the young woman who now called herself Marilyn Monroe. It was four long years before she finally landed a walk-on part in a gangster film called *Asphalt Jungle*. Her scenes were brief but electric, and moviegoers were enchanted by her beauty, her sensuality, and yet through it all a vulnerable innocence which she never lost. Her new fans and the studio bosses took notice. She won better and larger roles until, in 1953, scandal almost derailed her rise to stardom. It was revealed that she had posed nude for a calendar while she was a struggling starlet.

The studio heads awaited the national outcry of outrage and shock. But the criticism, amazingly, never came. There was something about Marilyn Monroe that everyone *liked,* no matter what. Bravely, she held a press conference to face belligerent reporters. Why had she posed naked? Monroe answered simply, "Because I needed the money."

One outraged female reporter apparently couldn't believe that Monroe had really been completely nude. "Didn't you have *anything* on at all when you posed?" she asked.

"Only the radio," Monroe said, smiling, and won everyone's hearts forever.

The controversy over the calendar catapulted Monroe to worldwide celebrity, a status she never lost. At the height of her fame, she received thousands of letters a week, dozens proposing marriage. According to *The New York Times,* Communists denounced her as a capitalist trick to make the American people forget how miserable they were.

But somewhere along the way things started to go wrong. In 1954 she married the most popular male athlete in the country, Joe DiMaggio, the baseball player. The marriage lasted only nine months. In 1956 Marilyn entered into another "dream" marriage, this one to the country's leading intellectual playwright, Arthur Miller. That dream also ended in divorce, in 1960. In fact, during the period of her greatest career success she had one personal disaster after another, ranging from miscarriages to failed marriages. She was told by doctors that she would never be able to have a child.

And then her acting career began a disastrous dip.

Two films, *Let's Make Love* and *The Misfits*, were box-office disappointments. And she started battling with her studio, 20th Century–Fox, over her next film, *Something's Got to Give*. She said she didn't want to do the picture. But now, for the first time, the studio, which used to be awed by its star, refused to bow to her wishes. The bitter message was clear. She was no longer a box-office phenomenon who could make her own rules.

Against that depressing background, the emergence of the two Kennedy brothers in her life must have seemed thrilling and magical. Shoddy Hollywood types may have been downgrading her, but at the same time she was rumored to be romancing the President of the United States. And then his brother the Attorney General began paying close attention to her, too, even visiting her Hollywood home.

Everything else in her life had turned sour. Strapped for cash, she was forced to give up her expensive cottage at the Beverly Hills Hotel and rent a modest home in Brentwood. She was taking so many tranquilizers that her psychiatrist became alarmed and had to put her on a pill-reducing program. And then, for one reason or another, the only bright light in her existence, the Kennedy connection, began blinking off, and her "distraught" calls to Robert Kennedy commenced—until, eventually, she couldn't reach him on the telephone.

At this point, Marilyn Monroe became so depressed that her psychiatrist, Dr. Ralph Greenson, insisted she hire a psychiatric nurse/housekeeper, Eunice K. Murray, to watch over her. And yet Monroe was fighting back. She had contacted the president of 20th Century–Fox about resuming work on the suspended motion picture. And she was actively considering offers to appear in a Broadway musical and a giant Las Vegas show for which she was guaranteed fifty-five thousand dollars a week.

So Mrs. Murray wasn't really worried when Marilyn Monroe came down to breakfast on August 4, 1962.

"Orange juice?" Monroe said with a smile. "Looks good." Dressed in a blue robe, she appeared surprisingly cheerful as she sat down across a table from the housekeeper, poured herself some juice and started chatting. But suddenly she asked Mrs. Murray a question that startled her. "Is there any oxygen in the house?"

Oxygen? Mrs. Murray thought. This wasn't a hospital. Why would oxygen be kept in a private home? She told Marilyn there was none and asked her why she wanted it. Marilyn said she was just curious.

Later that morning, Mrs. Murray telephoned Dr. Greenson to report the strange question, and Greenson said he would stop over later and talk to Marilyn about it.

At twelve noon, Mrs. Murray heard an argument in the hall. Pat Newcomb, Monroe's friend and press agent, had slept over the night before. And from what Murray could hear, Monroe was angry because Newcomb had removed her sleeping pills that night and Monroe hadn't been able to sleep. Now Mrs. Murray knew why Monroe, who usually slept until noon, had dropped into the kitchen for breakfast so early that morning. She heard the door slam as Newcomb left.

Dr. Greenson arrived in the afternoon and spent two

hours with his celebrated patient. He later reported that she was "confused and disoriented," but even up until the time of his own death several years later he never divulged Marilyn's reason for asking about oxygen.

Monroe, as usual, remained in her robe all day, spending most of that time in bed, talking on the telephone. Nevertheless, Mrs. Murray perceived no hint of a suicidal depression. In fact, at 7:30 P.M. Monroe was laughing and chatting on the telephone with Joe DiMaggio's son, Joe Junior.

Yet—and this was one of the strangest facts of the case—not thirty minutes after that happy conversation, Marilyn Monroe was dying.

We know this from the report of a telephone call made to Monroe at about eight that night. And the identity of the person who originated the call was another strange fact that has provided grist for the murder theorists. For it was Robert Kennedy's brother-in-law Peter Lawford.

Lawford didn't reveal the occurrence of that telephone conversation until a columnist who was a personal friend of Monroe's, Earl Wilson, got onto it. Twenty years later, in his *New York Post* column, Wilson wrote:

I've been remembering that weekend twenty years ago when Marilyn Monroe died mysteriously.

I remember very vividly the last words that anybody recalled her saying. Marilyn spoke them to Peter Lawford and he told them to me.

"Hey, Charlie," Lawford told Wilson he had said to Monroe, using a slang salutation of those days. He had telephoned her because she was supposed to join him and friends for a poker game and then dinner. His wife, Patricia, was on Cape Cod at the Kennedy compound.

According to Lawford, Monroe's voice was slurred. She said she couldn't come to dinner that night. Then she added words that were chilling: "Say goodbye to Pat, say goodbye to the President. Say goodbye to yourself because you've been a good guy."

Then, abruptly, she clicked off.

According to Wilson, Lawford said that when somebody says goodbye, "I think that's terminal." He thought she was dying, and, alarmed, he called his manager, who reminded him of a problem. "You're the brother-in-law of the President of the United States. You can't go over there." However, the manager apparently tracked down Milton Rudin, Monroe's agent, who called Monroe's house. It was then about 9:30 P.M., an hour and a half after her explicit "goodbye" conversation with Lawford.

Rudin inquired if Monroe was "all right." And Mrs. Murray knew that the light was still shining in Monroe's bedroom, and the cord to her telephone was still under the door. When Monroe was awake, and hadn't taken any pills, she always placed that telephone in another room for the night. So Mrs. Murray believed that Monroe was alive and well. And Rudin was reassured.

Mrs. Murray then went to sleep. But sometime in the middle of the night she awoke and noticed that the light was still burning in Monroe's room. Monroe never stayed awake that late. Was something wrong? She tried the door and found it locked. Monroe didn't answer her calls. Frightened, Mrs. Murray summoned Dr. Greenson, who broke a window with a poker from the fireplace to gain access to Monroe's bedroom.

They found the famous actress lying nude on her bed. In a poignant image that soon flashed around the world, Monroe's arm was outstretched, her hand on the telephone, as she lay in death.

Sergeant Jack Clemmons, watch commander at the West Los Angeles police station, logged a telephone call from Dr. Greenson reporting Monroe's death at 4:25 A.M. Sunday. Marilyn Monroe? he thought. It had to be joke. Instead of alerting a cruiser, as he normally would have done, he drove over himself to check the call.

Clemmons became suspicious immediately about the circumstances of Monroe's death. For one thing, the timing bothered him. Mrs. Murray said that they had found the body shortly after midnight, but Clemmons hadn't been called until 4:25 A.M. What had gone on in the meanwhile? Dr. Greenson said they had telephoned the studio and some of Monroe's business associates, but the sergeant did not believe that the calls could have taken four hours. Had someone been destroying evidence of foul play? he wondered.

That same morning I was reporting to work at the Medical Examiner's Office. Since I had joined the office as a deputy medical examiner, I had worked every Sunday and sometimes seven-day weeks because we were understaffed and the work was becoming backlogged. But on that morning I discovered something strange. Dr. Curphey had telephoned the office early to leave me a message. The note on my desk read, "Dr. Curphey wants Dr. Noguchi to do the autopsy on Marilyn Monroe."

I didn't think for a moment that he meant the movie star. I simply assumed it was another woman who happened to have the same name, perhaps because to me, as to almost all Americans, Marilyn Monroe was a phantom goddess of the screen, not a real person. In fact, my immediate thoughts were on a different track altogether. I felt sure that this autopsy was going to present a very special *scientific* problem. A more senior medical examiner would normally have performed the autopsy. And yet Dr. Curphey had made a unique call early on a Sunday morning assigning me to the job.

I was accustomed to requests to perform the more difficult scientific cases because I, alone on Dr. Curphey's staff, was a university faculty member, assistant professor of pathology for Loma Linda University Medical School, and Board-certified in both clinical and anatomic pathology. So, thinking that this namesake of Marilyn Monroe was going to give me trouble, I began to read the investigator's report on the death. The decedent was a female Caucasian, blue-eyed, five feet four inches, weight one hundred and fifteen pounds. She had been pronounced dead by a Dr. Engelberg. Many bottles of pills had been found on the table beside her bed, the report continued, including an empty bottle of Nembutal, a sleeping pill, and a partially empty container of another sleeping pill, chloral hydrate, a "knockout" pill, famous as the ingredient in Mickey Finns.

Under the heading "Additional Information," I

found my first real clue as to what had caused the death of this woman named Marilyn Monroe: "Dr. Hyman Engelberg, 9370 Wilshire Boulevard, had given refill on Nembutal day before yesterday." And farther along in the report I found this note: "Psychiatrist talked to her yesterday, very despondent."

On Friday the woman had purchased fifty Nembutals, and the next day the bottle beside her bed was empty. A routine suicide, I thought. But why, then, had Dr. Curphey assigned me to it? Perhaps because the autopsy wouldn't match the facts in the investigator's report. I knew from experience that autopsies often produce surprises. In fact, I believe that at least twenty percent of autopsies nationwide reveal that the initial theory of the cause of death is wrong.

At about nine-thirty that morning I changed into my white autopsy gown and walked down a narrow fluorescent-lit hallway to the autopsy room. I opened the door, the scent of formaldehyde immediately signaling the presence of death. In front of me, under fluorescent lights, was a long windowless room. Stainless-steel autopsy tables were evenly spaced across a tiled floor, each equipped with a water hose and drainage system, a sink, and a suspended scale. Pathologists dictated their observations into a tape recorder as the autopsy proceeded, or immediately afterward.

In retrospect, I should have been alerted at once to the fact that this was a "special case" by the presence of Deputy District Attorney John Miner, who was the liaison officer to our department.

The body on Table 1 was covered with a white sheet. I pulled it back slowly and stopped. For an instant I couldn't grasp the fact that I was looking at the face of the *real* Marilyn Monroe.

It was the first time in my young professional life that I had been emotionally affected by the sight of a decedent on an autopsy table. Forensic pathologists are, of course, inured to death; we must concentrate on our professional duties. And in my case, my mental attitude was additionally fortified by my Buddhist upbringing. Buddhism teaches that life does not end in death; instead it transfers to a new state of being and is, therefore, eternal.

But no one, professional or not, Buddhist or not, could have been unaffected by the sight of the beautiful Marilyn Monroe, so untimely dead. I couldn't help thinking that here, before me, was a person so incredibly fortunate in every way—from the endowment of an astonishing beauty to the talent, and drive, that had transported her from the ranks of factory workers to a woman who walked with presidents. All gone, so young.

And I realized what an awesome responsibility was ahead of me. I knew that everyone in the world would demand to know what had happened to the beloved Marilyn Monroe. With this responsibility in mind, I began my examination by searching painstakingly with a hand-held magnifying glass for any needle marks which would indicate that drugs had been injected. And I looked as well for any indication of physical violence.

I found no needle marks, and so indicated on the body diagram in the autopsy report. But, interestingly, I did find evidence which might have indicated violence—and I also marked that evidence on the diagram. On Monroe's lower left back was an area of slight ecchymosis, a dark reddish-blue bruise that results from bleeding into the tissues through injury. And the color of the bruise indicated that it was fresh rather than old.

A bruise means wreckage. Human tissue and blood vessels have broken under the impact of an external blow, and almost immediately the white blood cells, the "soldiers" of the blood, rush to the area to battle and contain this wreckage. They throw off protein digestive enzymes to start this process, and in so doing they change the color of the bruise in stages from dark reddish blue or purple to brown to light brown to yellowish brown to green and yellow, which is the last stage of the bruise before it heals. Thus pathologists can differentiate a fresh ecchymosis from an old one by examining its color.

Monroe's ecchymosis was dark, which meant it was fresh. But was it connected to her death, or recently incurred in some normal fashion, such as bumping into a table, for example? At the time of the autopsy, I did not believe it was a trauma connected to her death. Its location, just above the hip, and its slight size ruled against violence. I would have expected to find fresh bruises around the throat or skull if Monroe had been a victim of violence. Nevertheless, that fresh bruise on her hip still remains unexplained. And as a possible clue to violence, it is curious that most of the investigative reporters who later became interested in the case failed to pick it up.

The autopsy concluded, I wrote my report, which began:

EXTERNAL EXAMINATION. The unembalmed body
is that of a thirty-six-year-old, well-developed,
well-nourished Caucasian female weighing 117
pounds and measuring sixty-five and one-half
inches in length. The scalp is covered with
bleached blonde hair. The eyes are blue . . . a
slight ecchymotic area is noted on the left hip and
left side of lower back.

The report then went on to detail my internal examination of Monroe's cardiovascular, respiratory,
liver and biliary, hemic and lymphatic, endocrine, uri-
nary, genital and digestive systems. It was the section
on the examination of the digestive system that later
created all the controversy, leading conspiracy theorists to say it "proved" that Monroe was murdered.
For I found absolutely no visual evidence of pills in
the stomach or the small intestine. No residue. No
refractile crystals. And yet the evidence of the pill
bottles showed that Monroe had swallowed forty to
fifty Nembutals and a large number of chloral hydrate
pills. Therefore, the murder theorists claimed, Monroe must have been *injected* with the drugs that killed
her.

Just as important, in the subsequent controversy,
were the words I wrote at the bottom of the report (I
have italicized the important details):

Unembalmed blood is taken for alcohol and barbiturate examination. Liver, kidney, *stomach and
contents,* urine and *intestine are saved for further
toxicological study.*

But even as we waited for the toxicology laboratory to perform those tests, rumors of foul play in Monroe's death were already escalating. Monroe's friends and associates said that her career, which had been in a decline, was now on an upswing. So, they insisted, there was no reason for her to have suddenly committed suicide.

In the face of the controversy, Dr. Curphey decided to appoint a panel of psychological experts (quickly dubbed by newspapers "the Suicide Panel") to interview Monroe's relatives, friends and business associates to determine her psychological background. Was she capable of suicide or not? What were the factors, both tangible and psychological, influencing her behavior at the time she died?

A "suicide panel" was an innovation at that time which has since been copied widely around the nation. Almost always, in suicides, relatives are reluctant to admit, or believe, that their loved one took his own life. Uncertainty doubles their grief, while insurance companies have a vested interest in proving that it *was* suicide. So a suicide panel can help determine the truth and end controversy and confusion.

Unfortunately, it would not do so in the Monroe case, and for a special reason. The people questioned by the panel were promised confidentiality in order to encourage them to speak openly of intimate matters. And because of the confidentiality pledge, Dr. Curphey ordered that the reports of interviews and the panel's notes remain closed, as are all such confidential reports. A summary of these findings of the panel stating that Monroe's death was a suicide was included in the final autopsy report, but the fact that the interview notes have been kept secret for twenty years has, naturally, inspired a charge of an official cover-up.

The report from the toxicology laboratory would add even more fuel to the fire. It was delivered to me several hours after I completed my autopsy on Monroe's body, and as I read it a warning signal immediately sounded in my mind. Along with the liver, I had submitted specimens of blood for alcohol and barbiturate examination. In addition, I had forwarded other organs, including, most importantly, the stomach and its contents, and the intestine, for "further toxicological study." Now I instantly noted that the lab technicians had not tested the other organs I had sent them. They had examined only the blood and the liver.

Why this failure to perform all the tests, which is a routine procedure in the department today? The evidence found in the analysis of the blood and the liver, together with the empty bottle of Nembutal and the partly empty (forty pills missing out of fifty) bottle of chloral hydrate, pointed so overwhelmingly to suicide that the head toxicologist, Raymond J. Abernathy, apparently felt there was no need to test any further. Specifically, the blood test showed 8.0 mg.% of chloral hydrate, and the liver showed 13.0 mg.% of pentobarbital (Nembutal), both well above fatal dosages.

Still, I should have insisted that all the organs, including the contents of the stomach and segments of the intestine, be analyzed. But I didn't follow through as I should have. As a junior member of the staff, I didn't feel I could challenge the department heads on procedures, and the evidence had persuaded me as well as the toxicologists that Marilyn Monroe had ingested a sufficient amount of drugs to cause death.

When the Medical Examiner's findings were made public a few days later, the media were quick to pick up the omission and I wanted to rectify the mistake, but it was too late. A few weeks later, I asked Abernathy if he had stored the other organs of Monroe's body that I had forwarded to him. If so, we could still test them. I was disappointed when he said, "I'm sorry, but I disposed of them because we had closed the case," for I knew the media would charge a cover-up. I was right. A variety of murder theories would spring up almost instantly—and persist even today.

Operating on the assumption that Marilyn Monroe and a "diary" in her possession were somehow a threat to Robert Kennedy, the murder theorists began with the fact that Kennedy flew into San Francisco the day before Marilyn Monroe died, Friday, August 3, 1962. He was scheduled to make a speech to the bar association the following Monday night. But the murder theorists wondered why he arrived Friday for a speech three days later. FBI files showing that he and his family spent the weekend at the Gilroy, California, ranch of Mr. and Mrs. John Bates were dismissed as an FBI cover-up. They believed that Kennedy, instead, flew to Los Angeles to supervise the murder of Marilyn Monroe, and they pointed suspiciously to her telephone call from Peter Lawford, the implication being that there was only Lawford's word for what was really said in that last telephone call. Robert Slatzer reportedly interviewed a woman living on the same block as Monroe who claimed to have seen Kennedy and a man with a doctor's bag enter Monroe's house Saturday afternoon. And according to Slatzer's scenario, the man with the doctor's bag injected Monroe with the drugs that killed her.

"Evidence" that Kennedy directly participated in Monroe's murder was so bizarre that even other murder theorists rejected it. Many had a second theory. They believed that the murder was accomplished by some rogue elements in the CIA worried about information that Kennedy had given Monroe which she kept in a diary. And there was some supporting evidence for the existence of a diary. In 1962 Lionel Grandison was deputy coroner with clerical functions. It was he who signed Monroe's death certificate. And he claimed that he actually saw the diary in the Medical Examiner's Office, and that it disappeared the next day.

Other so-called "proof" that Kennedy had in some way participated in Monroe's death was offered by the famous wiretapper Bernie Spindel. Spindel had been gathering evidence against Kennedy on behalf of teamster union boss Jimmy Hoffa when his house was raided by the New York District Attorney's Office. Murder theorists pointed out that Kennedy was a New York senator at the time, and a friend of the New York County DA, Frank Hogan. They believed that Kennedy was behind the raid. Spindel's tapes, seized in the raid, were not returned, and Spindel officially filed a lawsuit to recover "tapes and evidence concerning the causes of death of Marilyn Monroe which strongly suggest that the officially reported circumstances of her demise were erroneous."

There was a third scenario offered by conspiracy

advocates, in which Kennedy was not the murderer but a potential victim of blackmail. In this version, killers slipped into Monroe's bedroom at night, injected her with drugs and forced her to telephone Kennedy at Peter Lawford's house and say that she was committing suicide. Kennedy was then supposed to rush to her side to rescue her—and find himself in a blackmail trap. But Kennedy didn't come, the trap failed, and Monroe was left to die.

All of these disparate murder theories shared one common thread: Marilyn Monroe had died by injection, not by swallowing pills. And to prove that charge, everyone pointed to the autopsy I had performed.

Allegations against my autopsy report came from several different quarters. Dr. Sidney B. Weinberg, then Chief Medical Examiner of Suffolk County, New York, now retired, was quoted by journalist George Carpozi, Jr., as saying, "The evidence points to all of the classic features of a homicide, much more so than a suicide." Another journalist, Anthony Scaduto, called it "one of the weirdest autopsy reports ever confected."

Norman Mailer was quoted about my motives: "The word was out to keep this thing a suicide, not to make it a murder. . . . If you're the coroner and you feel the official mood is to find evidence of a suicide, you wouldn't particularly want to come in with murder." But Slatzer went farthest of all in his attack. He claimed my official report was a fake. Allegedly, Los Angeles Police Department sources told him that the real autopsy report had been suppressed and a fraudulent copy made up by me and substituted.

For twenty years I had answered these criticisms only in general terms. But, now, on November 4, 1982, I had an opportunity to respond in detail under the questioning of the two assistant district attorneys officially investigating the death of Marilyn Monroe.

My autopsy findings on Monroe's digestive system had stated these facts (I've italicized the controversial details):

The esophagus has a longitudinal folding mucosa [the inner lining of the organ]. The *stomach is almost completely empty*. The *volume* is estimated to be *no more than 20 cc. No residue of the pills is noted*. A smear made from the *gastric contents* examined under the polarized microscope *shows no refractile crystals*. The mucosa shows marked congestion and submucosal petechial [pinpoint] hemorrhage diffusely. The duodenum shows no ulcer. The *contents of the duodenum* are also examined under the polarized microscope and *show no refractile crystals*. The remainder of the small intestine shows no gross abnormality. The colon shows marked congestion and purplish discoloration.

The investigators were interested in the answers to three questions stemming from this section of my report:

Question 1. The autopsy indicated that the stomach was "almost completely empty." How could the stomach be empty if Monroe had swallowed a great mass of pills?

Question 2. Dr. Weinberg, as quoted by Carpozi,

had stated, "With such a massive dose of barbiturates in her system, you must expect to find at least some partially digested capsules or tablets in the stomach, . . . some powdery material adhering to the stomach lining, and oftentimes—as in this case—you would expect a corrosive or raw, red appearance on the stomach lining." Why weren't there partially digested capsules, powdery material or a raw, red appearance on the stomach lining?

Question 3. If Monroe had swallowed a great quantity of yellow Nembutals, the yellow dye from the jackets of the capsules must have been found on the linings of her throat, esophagus and stomach. Why was no such yellow stain noted?

A fourth question concerned my external examination of Monroe's body. It was known that Dr. Greenson routinely injected Monroe the day before she died. Yet I had found no needle mark on her body. Why?

To answer the first question concerning the empty stomach, I began my explanation with a common experience. Sometimes when you eat exotic food that doesn't "agree" with you, you suffer from indigestion, which means that the stomach is rejecting the food and not passing it into the intestines easily. But when you swallow food like steak that you've eaten for years, there is no indigestion, because the food is passed smoothly on to the intestines.

So it is with pills swallowed by habitual drug users. Marilyn Monroe had been a heavy user of sleeping pills and chloral hydrate for years. Her stomach was familiar with those pills, and they were digested and "dumped" into the intestinal tract. In my experience with pill addicts, I expected to see no visible evidence of pills—a fact that only proved they were addicts, not that they were murder victims who had been injected.

In response to the second question and Dr. Weinberg's suggestion that, in addition to partially digested capsules and powder, one would also expect to find a raw, red appearance on the stomach lining, I replied that my autopsy report had stated that the "mucosa shows petechial hemorrhage diffusely." In other words, beneath the stomach lining (the mucosa), there was in fact widespread pinpoint hemorrhaging—the raw, red appearance Dr. Weinberg suggested.

I told the investigators that the third question, relating to the claim that the yellow dye from Nembutal should have stained the inner linings of the throat and the stomach, had obviously been raised by a layman who had no familiarity with Nembutal. As a medical examiner I had come to know this pill very well. It seemed to be one of the favorite drugs for those who wanted to commit suicide. And I pointed out that if you take a yellow Nembutal and touch it to your lips to moisten it, then rub your finger over the wet pill, you'll find that the yellow color does not rub off. Nembutal is made with a capsule whose color does not run when it is swallowed.

As to the fourth question, why no needle marks were found when it was known that Dr. Greenson had injected Monroe, I said that punctures made by fine surgical needles, such as Dr. Greenson used, heal within hours and become invisible. Only fresh punctures can be discovered. Dr. Greenson's injection had been made almost forty-eight hours before the autopsy. Therefore, I found no fresh puncture marks.

At the end of our interview, the assistant district attorneys told me that a chief medical examiner from another jurisdiction would be asked to interpret the original autopsy, along with my explanations of details. I was impressed by the thoroughness of their investigation into the twenty-year-old death.

Only three days after my visit to the DA's Office, I was driving through Brentwood on my way to Pasadena, where I was to teach a class in the art of Japanese cooking, one of my hobbies. I was only a mile or so from Marilyn Monroe's house when I heard the news announcer on the car radio say, "James Hall, who was an ambulance attendant in 1962, says that Marilyn Monroe was murdered right before his eyes. In an exclusive story in the newspaper the *Globe,* he was quoted as stating that he was actually reviving Monroe when he was pushed aside by a 'doctor' who injected a mysterious fluid directly into her heart and killed her."

Sprinklers on lovely green lawns, elegant palm trees along the boulevard, a lonely jogger moving happily in the sun—and another Marilyn Monroe murder story on the radio inside my car. I almost expected the announcer to say that the killer "doctor" was named Noguchi—and relaxed only when I heard that he had a mustache, longish sideburns and a pockmarked face. Not me.

Marilyn Monroe would have been fifty-six in 1982 —and yet the image of that lovely young actress, her hand stretching to the telephone in death, still seared the minds of Americans. Would the rumors and the speculations never stop? I wondered. Not only the "doctor" who supposedly injected Monroe, seen by the ambulance attendant, but even more outlandish tales. Sample: Monroe was drugged at Frank Sinatra's house in Palm Springs and her body flown to her house in Brentwood. (This one defied both logistics and logic.) Sample: Mrs. Murray had been on Peter Lawford's payroll ever since the day Monroe died, to keep her quiet about the real facts. Sample: Pat Newcomb, who slept in Monroe's house the night before she died, was hired by Pierre Salinger on behalf of the Kennedys, after Monroe's death, to silence her.

I sincerely hoped that when the DA's investigation was completed, these fantastic rumors, and many others, would be stilled. And perhaps the legitimate questions which still haunted her case would be answered.

The LA District Attorney's Office released the report of its investigation into the death of Marilyn Monroe in December of 1982, and its conclusion drew wide circulation.

Her murder would have required a massive, in-place conspiracy covering all of the principals at the death scene on August 4 and 5, 1962; the actual killer or killers; the Chief Medical Examiner-Coroner; the autopsy surgeon to whom the case was fortuitously assigned; and almost all of the police officers assigned to the case, as well as their superiors in the LAPD . . . our inquiries and document examination uncovered no credible evidence supporting a murder theory.

The report also noted: "The D.A.'s review was undertaken since there had been no D.A. investigation or full-scale case review in 1962 (although D.D.A. John Miner had been present at Dr. Noguchi's autopsy)."

I found the report fascinating on several levels. Personally, I hadn't known until I read it that John Miner, twenty years ago, had officially reported to the District Attorney's Office that I had performed a meticulous professional autopsy, including the use of a hand-held magnifying glass to search for needle marks. Miner was apparently unaware that all good pathologists do that in deaths where drugs are suspected, but I was gratified by his comment.

Of more professional interest to me was the report by the independent expert Dr. Boyd G. Stephens, Chief Medical Examiner/coroner in San Francisco. He concluded not only that the original autopsy was scientifically correct in 1962 but that "even the application of more advanced—1982—state-of-the-art procedures would not, in all reasonable probability, change the ultimate conclusions reached by Dr. Noguchi in 1962."

The DA's investigation was both conscientious and comprehensive. Almost every allegation had been followed up and found to be without basis so far as the DA's office was concerned, ranging from the mysterious missing "diary" to the "doctor" who had administered a "killing" shot, to the Spindel tapes, to Robert Kennedy's trip to LA on the weekend of Monroe's death.

But, of course, the investigation, two decades after the fact, could not answer the few legitimate questions that remained. There was no way, for example, it could determine the source of the bruise on Monroe's hip. Nor why she was laughing happily with Joe Di-Maggio, Jr., at 7:30 P.M. and dying only thirty minutes later. And what did the outstretched hand on the telephone mean?

I was also concerned that the persistent rumors of a cover-up had not been entirely dispelled. Journalists had reported that Monroe's FBI file, released to them under the Freedom of Information Act, had pages deleted, apparently for security reasons. And now, according to the DA's investigative report, the FBI files on Monroe that had been given to his office were also "heavily censored." I had to wonder. Why were the FBI files on a movie actress censored in the first place? What national-security concerns could be involved? And, more mysteriously, why in 1982 had the FBI felt that heavy censorship of her files was still necessary twenty years after Monroe died, even when the FBI was dealing not with journalists but with an official Los Angeles District Attorney's investigation? What is in Monroe's files?

I had another concern. The very man who had watched me perform the autopsy, John Miner, the DA's liaison with the coroner's office back in 1962, had presented a problem to the current DA's investigation. Miner had not only watched the autopsy, but he, alone among LA law officials, was granted an exclusive privilege by Dr. Greenson, Monroe's psychiatrist: he was allowed to listen to tape recordings of Monroe's own words in her sessions with Dr. Greenson.

According to the DA's report, Miner had pledged that he would never "repeat to anyone the details of Marilyn Monroe's statements and tape recordings given to Greenson during therapy sessions." But what he heard on the tapes, and his debriefing interview with Dr. Greenson, had convinced him that Marilyn Monroe had *not* committed suicide. The 1982 DA's report goes on to say:

Based on Miner's conversations with Greenson, he harbored serious questions regarding the finding that Miss Monroe's death was a suicide and felt compelled to express his reservations [in a memo to] the Chief Deputy District Attorney, [to] Dr. Curphey, and . . . others.

That was in 1962. Twenty years later the DA's investigators pressed Miner—and he apparently drew back. Now he said that what he had meant in 1962 was that Monroe had not committed *intentional* suicide. In Monroe's case, however, an accidental overdose of that magnitude was extremely unlikely. From my forensic experience with suicide victims, I believe that the sheer number of pills Monroe ingested was too many to swallow "accidentally." Thus, if Miner's evaluation in 1962 was correct, the only conceivable cause of Monroe's death was murder.

My final concern stemmed from the fact that the notes and interviews compiled by the suicide panel that studied Monroe's death remained confidential and were not released to the DA's investigators. Dr. Robert Litman was one of the psychiatrists on that panel, and I recently spoke to him again about the Marilyn Monroe case.

A founder of the Suicide Prevention Center and one of the nation's leading authorities on suicide, Dr. Litman told me that, from the information he and the other panelists received from friends and associates of Monroe, he had no doubt that she had killed herself. They discovered that she had tried to commit suicide twice before and was rescued at the last minute. Also, various associates had said she was extremely depressed just before her death and was acting strangely.

"Any chance of murder?" I asked him.

He shrugged. "The door to the bedroom was locked from the inside. They had to break a window to enter the room. And Mrs. Murray was in her room all evening only a little way down the hall from Monroe's."

What did happen in Marilyn Monroe's bedroom on the evening of August 4, 1962? In my opinion, Dr. Curphey's official conclusion stated the situation correctly (if evasively): "*probable* suicide." On the basis of my own involvement in the case, beginning with the autopsy, I would call Monroe's suicide "*very* probable."

But I also believe that until the complete FBI files are made public and the notes and interviews of the suicide panel released, controversy will continue to swirl around her death. The remaining questions will go unanswered, and no one will ever be able to say definitely what went on that evening which, in only thirty minutes, transformed Marilyn Monroe from a beautiful and talented actress, laughing and talking cheerfully on the telephone, to a dying movie star— and an undying legend.

4

Medical Examiner's Case No. 68-5731

Robert F.
Kennedy

At 10:15 P.M. on June 4, 1968, Senator Robert F. Kennedy opened the door of his fifth-floor suite in the Hotel Ambassador, Los Angeles, and slipped out into the corridor, surprising the three reporters down the hall. He leaned casually against the wall, arms folded, his blue suit rumpled, striped tie loose, and fielded the reporters' questions.

Downstairs in the Embassy Room the celebration of Kennedy's victory in the pivotal California presidential primary was already under way. But the situation was confused. The raw vote tallied so far indicated that Senator Eugene McCarthy, not Kennedy, was winning the primary. Still, the television networks unanimously projected Kennedy as the victor.

One of the men in the corridor with Kennedy was Jack Smith of the Los Angeles *Times,* who was neither a political nor a "hard news" reporter. So *his* question brought a smile to the Senator's face. "Did you catch the ninth wave?" Smith asked. To Californians, the ninth wave is thought to be that great breaker you're looking for in the surf that makes all the waiting worthwhile. It's the biggest, and often the most dangerous. That afternoon Kennedy had been to Malibu Beach with one of his sons. In reply to Smith's question, he said, "I guess that's where I got this," and touched a small purplish bump over his right eye. "I don't know the number of the wave, but I know the result."

Behind him in his suite were gathered his family, and friends such as ex-astronaut John Glenn and writer Budd Schulberg. Across the hall in a separate suite, his campaign staff followed the primary results. But Kennedy lingered with the reporters. Like his brother Jack, he had a congenial relationship with the working press and enjoyed bantering with newsmen. Finally, he finished the give-and-take with a typical Bobby Kennedy statement: "The only thing is to *win.*"

Then he turned to the door of his suite, a slim, short, brown-haired man above whom the three newsmen seemed to tower. The door opened, and the reporters heard someone say from inside, "McCarthy isn't conceding."

At ten-thirty that night, I was at home on Oxford Street in the Wilshire district of Los Angeles. Two lights were burning inside the house, one in the living room, the other in my bedroom upstairs. I was preparing for bed while my wife, Hisako, lingered below to continue watching the primary results on television.

The network forecasts that Kennedy would win the

California primary had brought the first cheering note into my life in weeks. My involvement in the Marilyn Monroe case had caused me to study the young Senator, and I admired him very much. To me, he and his late brother represented what I called the "Great America." I respected everything about them: their style, their leadership, their instinctive reaching out to all ethnic groups to say, Yes, you too are Americans.

It had been another sixteen-hour day for me at work. When Dr. Curphey retired in 1967, I became his successor, and the Los Angeles County Board of Supervisors appointed me Chief Medical Examiner. As with all county department heads, my appointment began with a six-month probationary period. Still, that made me, at forty, the first Japanese-American chief medical examiner in a major metropolitan jurisdiction in the United States. But as my probationary period was drawing to a close, I heard rumors that I might be replaced. The Board of Supervisors wanted one of their own in the job, not an "outsider."

Perhaps because I was troubled by those rumors, I was half awake when my wife came to bed. I asked her if Kennedy was still winning the primary, and she said McCarthy hadn't conceded but the networks were still firm in their projections that Kennedy would be the victor. A few minutes later that happy news helped me drift off to sleep.

I was awakened by the jangle of the telephone. What time was it? Who could be calling? I reached for the phone, knocking a teacup from the night table to the floor. And even before I placed the receiver to my ear, I could hear the excited voice of one of my deputies: "Dr. Noguchi, Dr. Noguchi."

"Yes."

"Something's happened. Something's happened. Kennedy has been shot!"

I immediately turned on the television set and saw the dreadful film replay of the shooting—people screaming, the close-up of the Senator's face as he lay on the floor of a hotel kitchen. And when I heard a paramedic say the Senator had been shot in the head, I felt a terrible foreboding and was more shaken than at any other time in my career.

Kennedy had won the California primary, and I prayed that he would live. But that night in my home the news of a gunshot to the Senator's head, which I knew to be potentially life-threatening, galvanized me in a professional way too. As yet, according to the television reporters, the police didn't have a full picture of what had taken place in that kitchen. A young man with a revolver had been apprehended on the scene, but were there other gunmen who had escaped?

Even as that thought flashed through my mind, Sandy Serrano, a Youth for Kennedy worker, appeared on the television screen. Breathlessly, she informed a reporter that she had been out on the terrace "for some air" during the Senator's victory remarks to the crowd inside when, suddenly, "a girl in a white polka-dot dress ran out of the hotel, shouting, 'We shot him.' "

That report caused a tormenting phrase to burn in my mind for the next forty-eight hours: "Don't let Dallas happen again."

In 1963 when President John F. Kennedy was assassinated, the Chief Medical Examiner in Dallas tried to take jurisdiction. Instead, the body was almost forcibly removed by Secret Service men and flown to Washington, where military doctors who were not qualified forensic pathologists completed the autopsy. They did the best they could, but, as the late Medical Examiner for New York City, Dr. Milton Helpern, said, "It was like sending a seven-year-old boy who has taken three lessons on the violin over to the New York Philharmonic and expecting him to perform a Tchaikovsky symphony. He knows how to hold the violin and bow, but he has a long way to go before he can make music."

Rushed by the White House staff, conducting their investigation thousands of miles away from the evidence they needed, the military doctors omitted some basic procedures, such as dissecting the neck wound. These omissions would form the basis for all kinds of rumors and conspiracy theories about the assassination for decades. FBI observers at the autopsy even misinterpreted the position of the neck wound in the autopsy report, stating that it was in the back rather than in the neck. And as a result, doubt had been cast on the forensic-pathology profession itself, which, in 1963, commanded little enough respect.

Now, tragically, a Kennedy brother might die in my jurisdiction. And it would be an awesome responsibility for our small and understaffed office, for it was essential, I thought, that this time the autopsy be carried out with absolutely no errors. So, at two o'clock that morning, I made a decision. I would call on the wisdom and resources nationwide of the still young and almost totally unknown forensic-medicine profession. If Kennedy should die, I would make this examination a national effort for pathologists.

It must have been about 3 A.M. when I telephoned the head of the agency which we pathologists call "our own INTERPOL." In 1966, Dr. William Eckert had founded INFORM, the International Reference Organization in Forensic Medicine, located in Wichita, Kansas. Today, years later, the agency is still unknown to the American public, but it is always working for them. Intelligence arrives daily in its headquarters from medical-examiner jurisdictions around America and is stored in computers so that forensic cases from cities thousands of miles apart can be compared, clues in mysterious deaths matched, and new medical innovations and scientific breakthroughs circulated to all pathologists for their use.

The call to Dr. Eckert, my first step in the impending case, was the beginning of a fateful journey which would carry me through many peaks and valleys. I had no way of knowing that morning that, after Senator Kennedy died, my autopsy would appear to contradict what every single witness, at least seventy in all, had seen with his own eyes in that crowded kitchen.

Or that the conflict between the eyewitness testimony and the autopsy would serve as the basis for review of the evidentiary portion of the case against the convicted killer, Sirhan Sirhan, in an attempt to overthrow his conviction. Sirhan had claimed that he brought the gun into the hotel kitchen but had no memory of what happened after that. It could not be denied that he had fired at the Senator, but his lawyer would allege that the *fatal* bullet was certainly triggered from another gun.

* * *

Ethel Kennedy smiled tentatively for the first time since the shooting. She stood beside her husband, holding a stethoscope against his chest. Dr. Victor Basiluskas, one of the attending physicians at Central Receiving Hospital, smiled with her.

"Will he live?" Mrs. Kennedy asked the doctor.

"At this minute he's doing all right. Let's hope."

Senator Kennedy had suffered cardiac arrest in the ambulance and had been brought into the hospital breathless, pulseless and lifeless. Basiluskas and his assistants had given him closed cardiac massage and then placed him in a heart-lung machine. There they administered oxygen, inserted a tube into his mouth to facilitate breathing, and injected adrenalin into the muscles.

Nothing happened. They waited. And miraculously, after ten or twelve minutes, there was a feeble breath and Kennedy's heart began to beat.

It was then that the doctor, on an impulse, handed Mrs. Kennedy the stethoscope, and her smile warmed him. Then he turned to an associate, Dr. Albert C. Holt, and told him that a neurosurgeon and a chest surgeon were waiting at "Good Sam." A few minutes later, Senator Kennedy was being rushed to the Hospital of the Good Samaritan, which was equipped with the most advanced technology in Los Angeles for dealing with the terrible wounds he had suffered.

Meanwhile, the swarthy young man in police custody told detectives his name was "John Doe." He was arrogant, uncooperative, and showed no remorse. But the gears of justice began to wear down his composure. In a few minutes the police discovered that the .22-caliber Iver Johnson pistol in his possession had been registered to a man named Munir Sirhan, of 696 East Howard Street, Pasadena. The man in custody was his brother, Sirhan Bishara Sirhan.

Back at the Hotel Ambassador, another witness told police that he too had seen the girl in the white polka-dot dress run out of the hotel. But he added a troubling detail. A "dark-complected" man had been running with her.

Only one dark-complected man, Sirhan Sirhan, was in custody. Had an accomplice escaped?

In the small hours of that morning, I had telephoned not only Bill Eckert in Wichita, but two other distinguished pathologists, Dr. Cyril Wecht in Pittsburgh and Navy Captain Bruce Smith in Washington.

Eckert had been insistent in his advice to me. "Take command of the examination right there in Los Angeles. Fight off any pressure to remove the body to Washington. No Dallas this time."

Then he had a shrewd idea. "This time bring Washington to *you.*"

"How?"

"Call AFIP and have their top pathologists fly to California to observe the autopsy."

Following up Eckert's suggestion, I contacted Captain Smith, director of the Armed Forces Institute of Pathology in Washington. He said that if Kennedy died, three AFIP experts would travel to Los Angeles aboard a supersonic military jet to participate in the autopsy. Then he said, "Do you mind if Pierre Finck is one of the team?"

I told him I wouldn't mind at all. Finck was one of the young doctors who had participated in President Kennedy's autopsy.

The irony—and tragedy—that the same doctor, by chance, might participate in the autopsies of two Kennedys was not lost on me. Nor was another irony. Six years before, I had performed the autopsy on Marilyn Monroe. And now I might perform the death examination of her alleged lover, Kennedy.

It was a strange turn of fate, but I had no time for thoughts of the past. Although I still devoutly hoped they would not be necessary, the first steps in my preparation for a historic autopsy had been accomplished. My invitation to AFIP had ensured that there would be total concurrence, and openness, at this autopsy, should it take place. My every move would be monitored by professional observers, every step corroborated. But the television reports of the girl in the white polka-dot dress and another young man running out of the hotel still worried me. What had she meant, shouting, *"We* killed him"? It seemed inevitable that we would have to investigate the possibility of conspiracy.

So I placed my last telephone call to Dr. Cyril Wecht, coroner of Allegheny County, Pennsylvania, an expert on political assassinations and the leading proponent among medical men of the theory of a second gunman in John F. Kennedy's assassination. Ten years later, in 1978, he would appear before Congress's assassination committee with charts and scientific evidence to demonstrate that four bullets had been fired at the President. As Lee Harvey Oswald had fired only three times, that meant, according to Wecht's evidence, that there had to be another gunman. The congressmen listened to Wecht politely but indifferently, and then called Wecht's fellow scientists on the panel, who blandly refuted his evidence in their testimony. It was only later, a few days before the assassination hearings concluded, that an acoustics scientist analyzed an auditory tape of a Dallas police radio broadcast during the assassination and announced that there *were* four shots, which meant there *was* a second gunman in Dealey Plaza. Thus Wecht may have been proven right.

But Wecht, although a feisty, articulate advocate, was not in any way a "fanatic." He went by the evidence, and he was politically astute. "Make certain you have full liaison with the political people," he told me. "If you don't, they'll blind-side you later if something comes up. Appoint a liaison with the U.S. Senate, because Bobby is a senator. And in Los Angeles, cooperate in every way you can with the Kennedy campaign staff."

Then, at 8 A.M. on June 5, after having been up all night, I reported to my office in the Hall of Justice and studied the step-by-step plan for the medical-examination procedure which I had prepared earlier. Still there was hope. The news bulletins from the Hospital of the Good Samaritan that morning were more optimistic. The main concern of the surgeons was not that Kennedy would die, but that his brain would be irreparably damaged. Horrible enough—but he would live.

Meanwhile, the people in sprawling Los Angeles were living their normal lives—and dying their too-often sudden and unexpected deaths. The daily influx of suicides, accident casualties, ODs, battered children and homicide victims was pouring into our department. And that terrible surge of death was still our prime responsibility.

I lost myself in the work process all that day. But then, at 8:30 P.M., the liaison officer at Good Samaritan called with the news I had dreaded to hear. "Senator Kennedy's brain waves have gone flat."

My hand went cold on the telephone. I knew that all hope was gone for this great American leader.

I called the AFIP experts in Washington immediately. They informed me that the Washington *Post* had a telephoto camera trained on the plane assigned to them at Andrews Air Force Base. When the aircraft took off, the *Post* would be the first newspaper to know that Bobby Kennedy was actually dying.

So far no official news of Kennedy's deteriorating condition had been disclosed. But all of my experience told me that now was the time for decision. Flat brain waves after a gunshot wound in the head can mean only one thing.

It would take the AFIP experts hours to fly across the country. I told them, "Go," and to hell with the Washington *Post*.

Outside Good Samaritan Hospital, at 3 A.M. on June 6, the crowds still stood in mute grief, their banners which read "PRAY FOR BOBBY" lowered. It was official. Senator Robert F. Kennedy was dead.

I remember the despairing mood of that crowd—the stricken faces of the young, a nun in tears holding a rosary—as I was ushered into the hospital. A security guard at the door to the autopsy room said hello to me and my two deputies in a low voice. Earlier, at 2 A.M., I had dispatched the first team from our office, including the investigator, the chief autopsy assistant and the photographer, with instructions to secure an autopsy room and make sure the hospital charts and X rays to be reviewed would be available, along with the surgeons who had tried to save Kennedy's life. The members of my staff, as well as the observers from the DA's office and Dr. Henry Cuneo, head of the neurosurgical team that had operated on Kennedy, were already assembled in the autopsy room when I arrived.

Senator Kennedy's body lay on a table, covered with a sheet. I removed the bandages on his head, then turned to the surgeons who had operated on Kennedy. The first thought in my mind was, Where are the hair shavings?

I knew that the scalp hair around the wound area which they had shaved off Kennedy's head before the surgery might contain critical evidence. So I instructed one of my investigators to rush to the operating room to see if the hair shavings were still there. They were found in little clumps which had been retained by the hospital staff. My investigator carefully placed them in a coroner's evidence envelope.

With the hair shavings retrieved, I was ready to turn my attention to the body. But my emotions at that moment led me to make an extraordinary request, surprising my fellow pathologists, who knew it was not normal procedure. It would be the only instance in the thousands of autopsies I have performed when I asked that the deceased's face be covered with a towel. Only then could I perform my work professionally, unshaken by my feelings for Kennedy. And I observed a moment of silence, head bowed, a Japanese custom showing respect for the deceased.

We began the autopsy at the feet and worked up to

the head, instead of the reverse procedure, which is more common. I believed that this methodology, conducted slowly and patiently, would result in a more complete and thorough examination of the victim. Sometimes too much attention is paid to the wound area, and important evidence elsewhere may be overlooked.

In fact, the first wound I found was an old one. The chief radiologist at the hospital, Dr. Robert Scanlan, told me that Kennedy's medical records showed that he had fractured his left leg while skiing. And as I noted that fracture, a picture flashed through my mind of the vibrant, active Kennedy, climbing rugged mountains, skiing snowy slopes, shooting turbulent rapids in a Colorado river with his family. He had loved life so much.

The first fresh wound I studied was what we call a through-and-through gunshot wound. The entry was underneath and slightly to the back of the right armpit. The bullet had traveled at an angle, exited through the front right shoulder and been lost.

The second wound I examined was also under the armpit, about an inch from the first. But, surprisingly, this bullet had not traveled in the same direction as the other, which had exited from the front. Instead, it had traversed the back, side to side, and had lodged in the soft tissue of the paracervical region at the level of the sixth cervical vertebra (the spinal column at the back of the lower neck). With my right index finger and thumb I removed a deformed .22-caliber bullet. I had retrieved the first tangible evidence that police could use to identify the gun.

But I was not so fortunate in probing the path of the

all-important bullet that had caused Kennedy's death. The bullet had entered the skull an inch to the left of Kennedy's right ear, in what is known as the mastoid region, and shattered. The tiny fragments could be analyzed to reveal what type of ammunition had caused the wound, in this case, a .22. But such small metallic bits could not be matched definitively to Sirhan's gun. That meant that other evidence would be needed to establish that Sirhan Sirhan was in fact the assassin.

Under the watchful eyes of my associates and all the other observers in the room, I completed the most meticulous autopsy I had ever performed. But in Kennedy's death, in one of the most ironic twists in my career as a medical examiner, the very thoroughness of my tests served only to give credence to a conspiracy theory. As John McKinley later wrote in *Assassination in America:* "Compared with . . . conjectures, the riddles of the physical evidence weighed heavy as gold. Dr. Thomas Noguchi's thorough autopsy provided the most basic data, which paradoxically gave impetus to several questions about the assassination."

And in another ironic twist, it was those clumps of hair retrieved only at the last minute from the operating room that would lead in part to conjecture that Sirhan Sirhan had *not* fired the fatal bullet.

The day after the autopsy, a criminalist from the Los Angeles Police Department appeared at my office door. "Dr. Noguchi, we've found something in those little hair shavings."

"What?"

"Gunpowder residue. Not only metallic elements, but what could be soot."

"Soot?" I sat straight up. Only that morning, the police had informed me that all the witnesses to the assassination had reported that Sirhan Sirhan had been at least a yard away when he fired at Kennedy. But if there was soot in the scalp hair, that meant a gun had been triggered within *inches* of the head.

When a gun is fired, many different substances are discharged from its muzzle: the bullet and metallic fragments, unburned grains of powder, and burned grains of powder which we call soot, followed by a metallic spray of primer. The gas which contains the soot (carbon particles) is extremely light. It travels only a few inches. The unburned powder grains, which are heavier, travel farther, from one to two feet. And the bullet and metallic elements, naturally, travel a great distance because of their weight.

I examined carefully the infrared photographs of the hair shavings which the criminalist from the LAPD now showed me. They revealed a dust made up of metallic elements, with some carbon particles too— the telltale soot. But was there any other evidence to indicate that the fatal shot had been fired only a few inches away? I remembered that unburned powder grains were tattooed in a circular pattern on Kennedy's right ear. But if there had been soot on his ear, it was washed away when a surgical nurse scrubbed it.

Because of the soot in the hair, I believed that the muzzle distance of the fatal shot had been from one to three inches away. But I decided that a ballistics test would be necessary to determine the precise distance. And I conceived a test that would attempt to duplicate the tattoo pattern of unburned-powder stains on Kennedy's right ear.

That afternoon, a lab technician was startled by my request. "Seven pigs' ears?"

Explaining the reason for my request, I then asked him to affix the pigs' ears to padded muslin configurations, each simulating a skull. We would then take the "skulls" to the Police Academy shooting range for a unique ballistics test which I would supervise.

The next day at police headquarters, a plainclothes officer approached the "skulls." I asked him to fire at each of them, beginning with a firm contact shot, then moving back to a quarter inch, a half inch, one, two, three and four inches. I put on earmuffs while one of my staff measured the distance for each shot. Every time the marksman pulled the trigger and a bullet plowed through a muslin "skull," the sharp sound pierced the protection over my ears. *Crack! Crack! Crack!* The marksman moved down the line, carefully, until he had completed seven shots.

At three inches from the right mastoid area, I discovered we had a perfect match of the tattoo pattern of unburned-powder grains on Kennedy's right ear. At that distance, the shape of the entrance wound was also duplicated, and it accounted for the carbon particles found in Kennedy's hair. I now knew the precise location of the murder weapon at the moment it was fired: one inch from the edge of his right ear, only three inches behind the head. But I also realized that this evidence seemed to exonerate Sirhan Sirhan. Eyewitnesses are notoriously unreliable, but this time their sheer unanimity was too phenomenal to dismiss.

Not a single witness in that crowded kitchen had seen him fire behind Kennedy's ear at point-blank range.

But even apart from the autopsy findings of a close-range wound, there was other evidence to challenge the belief that Sirhan Sirhan had acted alone. For example, four bullets were fired at Kennedy; three of them struck him, and one passed harmlessly through his clothing. Five persons behind Kennedy were also struck by bullets, which were recovered in their bodies. And three bullet holes were found in the ceiling. Thus, the tracks of twelve bullets were found at the scene, and Sirhan's gun contained only eight. Police believed that the extra tracks could be accounted for by ricochets. But to the day he died (the victim of an assassin's bullet himself), Allard Lowenstein, one of Senator Kennedy's strongest supporters for the Presidency, said that Sirhan had not acted alone. And such professional homicide investigators as Vincent Bugliosi, the deputy DA who convicted the Manson killers, said that more than enough evidence existed to justify reopening the investigation.

What was the truth?

There was excitement in the kitchen of the Hotel Ambassador, crowded on the night of June 4, 1968, not only with hotel employees but with young Kennedy campaign workers—and strangers. Word had just flashed from the ballroom that Senator Kennedy was going to pass through the pantry on his way to the rear exit of the hotel, instead of leaving through the ballroom.

White-hatted chefs, Mexican busboys, and college students, alerted by the news, pushed and shoved their way into the serving pantry, a closed hall six feet wide and about fifteen feet long. A steam table with stacks of trays dominated one side of the room; a large ice machine stood across from it. The employees and the campaign workers arranged themselves roughly in two lines, between which Kennedy would walk.

"Here they come!" someone shouted.

Karl Eucker, a burly maître d', was the first man to appear. He led Robert Kennedy and his wife, Ethel, into the pantry, and Kennedy grinned shyly as he acknowledged the applause. There were no security guards; all had been taken by surprise by Kennedy's decision to leave the hotel through the back door and had been left behind in the ballroom.

A kitchen chef in the row of spectators to Kennedy's left said, "You're going to win, Mr. Kennedy!"

Kennedy smiled, stopped to shake the chef's outthrust hand . . .

BANG!

The sound of a shot cracked through the room. What was happening?

First, what did the eyes of the onlookers see? Kennedy threw up his right arm. More shots were heard. Then witnesses observed a young, dark-complected man half crouching in front of Kennedy from three to six feet away, firing a pistol with two hands.

"Kennedy backed up against the kitchen freezer as the gunman fired. He cringed and threw his hands up over his face." That was the eyewitness report of Boris Yaro, a Los Angeles *Times* reporter, and it almost perfectly matched the image that all of the other witnesses observed: Sirhan shot and fatally wounded Kennedy openly and brazenly from in front.

But forensic evidence suggested that the shooting occurred in a different way. An instant after Kennedy entered the pantry, a gun appeared three inches from the back of his head, fired, then disappeared. Kennedy threw up his right arm and started to turn. Other shots were fired, and one bullet plowed through the clothing over his shoulder, missing flesh. Two more missiles struck his right armpit, but traveled in different directions, because he was turning. One traversed back to front at an angle; the other passed side to side, lodging in the back of his neck.

That slow-motion forensic re-creation of the scene could mean only one of two things: (1) either Sirhan lunged toward Kennedy and fired, a move unseen by anyone, and then, as Kennedy spun, lunged *back* to fire from farther away, a second move also invisible to all, or (2) a second gunman triggered the first shots up close, ducked away, and then Sirhan fired the other bullets from three feet away as Kennedy turned.

I have always believed it is perfectly possible that Sirhan could have made that lunge back and forth without being seen by any of those witnesses. My experience with homicides as a medical examiner has shown me over and over again how, and why, witnesses in a crowd in such a situation don't always see the truth. Their eyes are totally glued to the celebrity. It is only reluctantly, and as realization of something wrong sets in, that they move their eyes away from the celebrity and look elsewhere. In other words, the witnesses may not have seen what actually happened that night. But there are two factors that challenge that supposition—one forensic, the other the testimony of a particular witness.

Forensically, we see, after the fatal shot, three bullets traveling in different directions through Kennedy's body. That means that Kennedy was spinning. But it also means that time was consumed as he turned. Witnesses had more seconds than usual to take their eyes off the celebrity to observe Sirhan shooting. And within that extended time span, when they did see him, he was already three feet away from Kennedy, not lunging from behind him.

Secondly, the testimony of the most strategically placed witness is daunting. Karl Eucker, the maître d', led the Kennedys into the pantry. He was the man actually standing between Sirhan and the Senator. In fact, it was Eucker, not Roosevelt Grier or Rafer Johnson, who actually grabbed Sirhan and first wrestled him onto the steam table. Eucker was perfectly placed, and even years later he insisted, "I told the authorities that Sirhan never got close enough for a point-blank shot. Never!" Then he warned that an investigation of a second-gunman theory would get nowhere. "It was decided long ago that it was to stop with Sirhan," he said, "and that is what will happen."

If, in fact, Sirhan did *not* lunge at Kennedy, unseen by anyone, and then draw back to continue shooting, is it possible that there was a second gunman and that Sirhan, consumed with hatred for Kennedy, had agreed to jump into the middle of the room and start firing wildly to divert attention from the real killer?

In 1970, in another twist in the history of this case, my own attorney, Godfrey Isaac, to my surprise, represented Sirhan Sirhan in the judicial review of his conviction, the basis for which was summed up in the affidavit of an investigator Isaac hired, William W.

Harper, a consulting criminalist to the Pasadena, California, Police Department and a former Naval Intelligence officer. His affidavit's conclusion:

> It is evident that a strong conflict exists between the eyewitness accounts and the autopsy findings. This conflict is totally irreconcilable with the hypothesis that only Sirhan's gun was involved in the assassination. The conflict can be eliminated if we consider that a *second* gun was being fired from Firing Position B concurrently with the firing of the Sirhan gun from Firing Position A. It is self-evident that . . . Sirhan could not have been in both firing positions at the same time. No eyewitness saw Sirhan at any position other than Firing Position A where he was quickly restrained by citizens present at that time and place.

Sirhan's conviction was upheld. But scientific evidence of soot and divergent bullet angles, and a host of witnesses who did not actually see Sirhan fire the fatal shot, all seemed to indicate there may have been a second gunman. Moreover, even the most sophisticated forensic techniques were unable to prove that the fatal bullet was fired from Sirhan's gun.

And yet . . .

My own professional instinct instructs me that Sirhan somehow killed Senator Kennedy alone. He has always insisted he acted alone, and he kept a diary in which he wrote, "RFK MUST DIE." But instinct and even educated guesses are not enough. Forensic science must concern itself only with the known facts.

And I believe that the Kennedy assassination must go down in the history of forensic science as a classic example of "crowd psychology," where none of the eyewitnesses saw what actually happened. But until more is positively known of what happened that night, the existence of a second gunman remains a possibility. Thus I have never said that Sirhan Sirhan killed Robert Kennedy.

Perhaps the whole truth will never be known. And that is a dilemma that sometimes confronts modern forensic science—a dilemma that in the Kennedy case began through the discovery of particles of soot in Kennedy's own hair. The night of his assassination, Robert Kennedy did indeed seem to be riding the ninth wave. It bore him upward to a great political victory, then plunged him to his death. And thinking of him today, I remember what he said to the reporter Jack Smith about the ninth wave. Bobby Kennedy's reply must be my own as a forensic scientist when I consider the circumstances of his assassination: "I don't know the number of the wave, but I know the result."

5

The
Hearings

The Kennedy autopsy report was hailed by forensic pathologists across the nation as "a prototype for all autopsies of legal significance." It was an important victory for my profession. At last forensic science was being accorded the attention and respect it deserved. And I was more than gratified when the Los Angeles County Board of Supervisors voted to install me as permanent Chief Medical Examiner after all.

For me, it was the realization of a dream, and I felt I was now in a position to make another dream come true: the expansion and modernization of the Medical Examiner's Office. We were still housed in the basement of the Hall of Justice, where it was only a slight exaggeration to say that the rats outnumbered the microscopes. We needed larger space and a larger staff

—in short, a larger share of the county budget. And I set out to get it.

Lin Hollinger, the Chief Administrative Officer, was in charge of the day-to-day administration of the county. It was he who ruled on the budget requests from my office. And when I told him that we needed not only a large infusion of new personnel to cope with the escalating case load, but also an entire new building, a Forensic Science Center which would cost more than a million dollars, he felt that my demands were excessive. He seemed to be opposed even to my smaller requests. So I committed the cardinal sin of bureaucracy. Bypassing my immediate superior, I went directly to the Board of Supervisors. And I soon found, to my dismay, that I had another battle on my hands, a battle that would revolve around not my professional competence but my personality.

Hollinger fired the first shot. One day as I sat with him in his office, I remember, he abruptly drew a finger across his throat in a slitting gesture and said, "You'll never embarrass me again."

The gesture was so sudden that I was taken aback, and I asked him what I had done. He replied hotly that I had gone over his head with a personal request to the Board of Supervisors to hire more investigators. What was worse, the Supervisors had approved the request over Hollinger's objection, and that, he said, was intolerable. In fact, the finger across the throat symbolized it all. I was through. Finished.

I knew that the Supervisors, as well as the Administrator, were annoyed by my constant requests for appropriations, but I couldn't believe that my job was in jeopardy simply because I hadn't gone through channels. There must be another reason.

Hollinger confirmed that suspicion. "You'll have to go," he said, holding up a file in his hand. "We've had too many complaints about you. Everyone is against you, the doctors and everyone. If you don't resign, we'll file charges against you."

I was startled by his words. How could "everyone" be against me? I hadn't been in the job long enough to create enemies, I thought. I was so curious that I impulsively reached for the file, but Hollinger quickly withdrew it and stuffed it into a drawer. Then he said that the Board of Supervisors all agreed with him that I must go. And as a lure for me to resign, they would appoint me chief pathologist at Rancho Los Amigos Hospital, at the same pay I was now receiving.

I told him I liked my present job, but I left his office a confused and beaten man.

My first reaction was to send the Board my letter of resignation. I thought there was no alternative. But later, at the prodding of a friend, David Smith, I changed my mind. At the eleventh hour before acceptance of the resignation took place, I sent a telegram to the Board withdrawing it.

When I refused to resign, I was fired, and no fewer than sixty-one charges were filed against me, perhaps the most lurid ever brought against a public servant, and the newspapers loved it. Suddenly a little bureaucratic controversy in Los Angeles was news around the world.

Here are just a few of the charges:

I threw a shoe at a black chauffeur.

I said I wanted 707 jets to crash so that I could

perform the autopsies on the victims and become famous.

I smiled in the middle of mass disasters.

I wanted Los Angeles Mayor Sam Yorty to die in a helicopter accident.

I "reveled" in the publicity I attracted after the Robert Kennedy assassination.

I threatened another employee with a knife.

I described to associates a splendid vision I had in which a fully loaded jet liner collided with a hotel "and amidst the flames, I, Thomas T. Noguchi, stood, and the press was there."

I said I wanted to perform a live autopsy on Lin Hollinger.

In sum, the implication was that I was mentally disturbed—crazy. I was furious, but at the same time I thought it would be hopeless to fight back—indeed, suicidal. The Board would produce witnesses to "support" the charges, and my reputation would be destroyed. Even if I could prove that the charges were false, I would be indelibly stamped as some sort of madman who "prayed" for mass deaths and disasters. I would never be able to find another job in my field.

It was then that a man literally saved my life. I went to see attorney Godfrey Isaac at the suggestion of a friend, but I told him I felt it was no use to resist, because the Board was determined I should go. Isaac disagreed. Those outrageous charges had been filed *and* published, he said. If I didn't fight them, the whole world would believe that the accusations were true. In effect, I had no choice but to resist.

Isaac was a short, dapperly dressed individual with an informal, engaging personality. I had been told that he was a brilliant trial lawyer, a master of the difficult art of cross-examination, and a tough all-around battler for his clients' rights. I liked him immediately, and when he agreed to act in my defense I sensed for the first time a small ray of hope.

As he grew more familiar with the circumstances of my case, Isaac would become convinced that there was an underlying motive for the actions of the Board of Supervisors. "It seemed to me," he later wrote, "that Noguchi was a target because of plain, old-fashioned prejudice. They were out to get him because he was Japanese, that's all there was to it."

I did not want to believe that. But Isaac convinced me that my professional reputation was at stake. I had to fight to save that. We took my case to the Civil Service Commission of Los Angeles. And thus the stage was set for what the newspapers would call perhaps the most sensational hearing in Los Angeles history.

As we began preparations for my defense, the first problem was money to pay the legal fees. I had very little of my own, and friends suggested that the Japanese-American community might come to my support. That proved to be an unrealistic hope, for we discovered that many people felt that I had embarrassed the Japanese-American community. In sum, I realized, they believed that the charges against me they had read in the newspapers were true. So, because of lack of funds, my legal defense became a family affair. Hisako and I withdrew our entire life savings from the bank. And Isaac's wife, Roena, became an investigator.

The hearing before three Civil Service Commissioners was set to begin on May 12, 1969. That day a huge crowd filled the hearing room, eager to witness the action. I sat with Isaac at a defense table, with all eyes —and a television camera—on me. The television people had requested, and received, permission to cover this "trial" in full.

Martin Weekes, the deputy counsel for the county, stood up to make his opening statement. It rocked the court, not only because of its content but because his voice was actually choked with emotion as he poured out the charges he intended to prove. They were incredible.

Weekes claimed that I had danced in my office as Senator Kennedy lay dying, saying "I'm going to be famous . . . I hope he dies . . . because if he dies, then my international reputation will be established." And when two giant airliners collided near Los Angeles, I hadn't been satisfied with the numerous corpses stacked in the morgue, because, according to Weekes, I had fixed a magic figure, fourteen thousand, as the number of deaths I wanted processed in my first twelve months as Chief Medical Examiner. That was when, also according to Weekes, I had "prayed" that a fully loaded jet liner would plummet into a hotel and I would stand "amidst the flames . . . and the press was there."

Then Weekes revealed why his voice was throbbing so emotionally. Just that morning he had heard that my black deputy, Lewis Sawyer, had died. I had worked Sawyer, Weekes said, "until he dropped. And drop he did." Only as an afterthought did he mention that Sawyer had actually died of cancer. And Isaac whispered to me, "Weekes is all choked up because he forgot to add cancer to the other sixty-one charges against you."

Herbert McRoy, my administrative chief of staff, was the county's first witness, called to substantiate the charge that I wanted 707s to fall from the sky. He said he had heard me utter that wish just after two helicopter crashes in May 1968, adding that the statement had been made in front of him and my secretaries on many occasions in the office.

It was not enough that I prayed for accidents. When McRoy finished, an investigator named Day testified that at the height of an influenza epidemic I had walked through a morgue stacked with bodies, looking joyous. He stated that I had said happily to him, "You like it?" And according to Day, whenever there were terrible tragedies, ranging from the helicopter crashes to the Kennedy assassination, I always had a look of "elation" on my face. "This did not," he testified, "seem to be appropriate for the situation involved."

Day's testimony about my "elation" was so absurd that Isaac spent little time on cross-examination. But later he would produce our own expert witness, who brought laughter to the hearing room by saying it was not surprising that a Japanese looked "elated" during a disaster: "They smile no matter what happens."

An ex-secretary, Eleanor Schmidt, testified next and said that I referred to Orientals as "Yellow Submarines." Then she described a vivid scene. One day, she alleged, I took a knife from my belt, slashed a sheet of paper in two, then said to her ominously, "I could use this knife for an autopsy on the living—and perhaps an autopsy on Mr. Hollinger."

According to another secretary, Ethel Fields, I was a racist. I "hated all niggers, Jews, and Japs," she said. As I myself am Japanese, the remark brought chuckles even from one of the presiding commissioners.

I was also a publicity hound. Fields testified that I instructed her to activate my beeper device when I was making a speech, so that I would look important. And not only that. I was profane.

Q. What words did he use, ma'am?
A. Well, frequently he said "goddam it," and then other times he said "son of a bitch." And, once when he received a letter he was upset about, he said, "Goddam son-of-a-bitch pissing peters."

Laughter in the hearing room.

Q. Did you find his language offensive?
A. Well, I was rather shocked.

Fields also stated that I had waited gleefully for Senator Kennedy to die, and she repeated to the commissioners what the newspapers were now calling "Noguchi's famous prayer for disaster." "Relative to the helicopter crashes," she testified, "he said that . . . he hoped other helicopters would crash, and that this would be in his jurisdiction. And that . . . the press would be there and . . . he would become well known internationally and nationally."

Q. Then with reference to the other aircraft crashes, what statements did he make?

A. He also said that he hoped some other large jets would crash so that he could handle the case.

Testimony about Kennedy and the air crashes coming from one of my own secretaries was damning. But on cross-examination Isaac elicited information which surprised even him.

Q. From whom did you get what you call the full story [of my statements about Kennedy and the air crashes]?

A. Well, partly from the papers.

Isaac stopped. Usually in control of a cross-examination, he had obviously been caught off guard.

Q. You mean that a good part of your testimony that you have given here is based upon what you have read in the newspapers?

A. Yes, and what I have obtained from Mr. Weekes [the county counsel]—what they have told me.

Fields's testimony, seemingly direct from her own experience, had, instead, apparently come from the newspapers and from the county's attorney.

Q. Did you read about the so-called prayer for disaster in the Los Angeles metropolitan dailies?

A. I don't take the Los Angeles *Times*. All I take is [a local paper].

Q. Did you read in the newspaper about Dr. Noguchi's statement about air disasters?

A. Yes, sir.

Q. Did you read in the newspaper about Dr. Noguchi's behavior about Kennedy?

A. Yes, sir.

Fields's testimony was a shocker to the commissioners—and symbolic of the turn the hearing was taking in my direction. Then witnesses who testified in my favor began trooping to the stand: secretaries who said that I was "a really great boss," and that I even paid for their Christmas office party out of my own pocket; a dozen employees who stated under oath that they had never heard me wish for disasters.

Was I crazy? Dr. Frederick Hacker, a respected psychiatrist who had studied my case in preparation for the hearing, was asked, "Is Dr. Noguchi 'normal'?"

"No, not normal," Dr. Hacker replied. "Supernormal. It's certainly not normal for a man to do all the things he has managed to do. . . . Dr. Noguchi may be unusual in some areas, in his ability, in his accomplishments, and, yes, in some of his customs and habits. But that is not abnormal."

A pathologist was called to the stand to testify about my work on the Robert Kennedy autopsy. "[It] was what I would call a complete autopsy," he said, "as complete as a pathologist can make one. It was highly organized."

"Object!" Weekes's voice cut through the hearing room. "May we approach the bench, Your Honor?"

I sat there watching as both attorneys went into a huddle with the three commissioners. Isaac told me later what had happened. Weekes had demanded that the commissioners not listen to our witness's testimony about the Kennedy autopsy. His reason? The autopsy report had been placed in evidence at Sirhan's trial, and a courtroom battle over it might lead to an "international incident." In truth, Isaac told me, Weekes didn't want my skill extolled and was using a fake issue, national security, to keep it out of the hearing.

Obviously, the county's case against me was crumbling, and the Kennedy-autopsy issue, in which we triumphed, completed the rout. The media, sensing that the county's actions had become more and more unfair, came over full square to my side. As did the Japanese-American community, which formed a group called JUST—Japanese United in Search of Truth—to help raise money for my legal defense.

After that, every day in court was a fiesta. I had become a hero to many of the people who crowded the hearing room. Meanwhile, the parade of witnesses testifying in my defense continued as Isaac sought to show that the county's charges against me were based on simple misunderstandings and had no substance in fact. Charles Maxwell, the chief of the mortuary division, testified that he personally had heard the celebrated prayer for a 707 accident.

Q. When Dr. Noguchi . . . had that discussion about a [707] crashing, you recognized that he

was being facetious, didn't you? . . . You
didn't take him seriously, did you?

A. No, of course not.

Another witness went on to explain, "We pathologists have senses of humor that might not be understood by nonpathologists. In the line of work that we
are engaged in, dealing with death and disease so
much, a sense of humor is more or less a survival kit
for us. This is a sort of gallows humor or . . . grave-
yard humor, as other individuals have termed it."

Q. This is common practice among pathologists?
A. Yes, it is. I'm afraid sometimes that if the remarks we made—if the general public were to
hear them, they may be misunderstood.

Finally, as a rebuttal witness, the county unleashed
its biggest gun: Lin Hollinger, the county's Chief Administrative Officer, who had inspired the hearing in
the first place. He testified, as Isaac commented, like
a god from Olympus. His voice was authoritative, his
accusations shook the room. The impression he gave
was that firing a local coroner was just a nasty little
bureaucratic chore for him. No big deal. As for the
charges against me, each and every one of them was
true. How did he know? His people had investigated
every allegation and confirmed its accuracy. And even
one of them, if proven true, was sufficient grounds to
fire me, let alone sixty-one. As far as he was concerned, Hollinger said, "The firing of Dr. Noguchi
was absolutely justified."

Did he have any personal animosity toward Noguchi? No. What about the throat-slitting gesture? It never happened, Hollinger said.

The commissioners were impressed with this dignified executive, renowned in the county for his straightforward if sometimes blunt approach. But in a brilliant cross-examination Isaac found the chink in his armor.

"Mr. Hollinger," he asked, "isn't it true that you recommended the discharge of Dr. Thomas T. Noguchi because you believed he was too emotionally disturbed to perform autopsies?"

"Yes, that's true," Hollinger replied.

"Mr. Hollinger, isn't it true that when you asked Dr. Thomas T. Noguchi to resign, you offered him a post at Rancho Los Amigos Hospital as a pathologist?"

"Yes, I did."

Isaac shocked Hollinger with the next question. "Do you have any reservations about sending a person who is too mentally ill to operate on dead bodies to a job where he operates on people who are still *alive?*"

Hollinger, caught in the contradiction, seemed dumbstruck. And I believe it was then that the commissioners asked themselves definitively, "Why was Noguchi really fired?" Certainly I may have been a little flamboyant, even a "publicity hound," an extrovert in a profession which seems to call for quiet serenity. Certainly I had a sense of humor which could seem out of place in a coroner's office. And if I had irritated the Board of Supervisors with my excessive demands, I was ambitious both for myself and for my department. But whatever the quirks in my personality, the county had been unable to cast a single doubt on my professional competence.

On July 31, 1969, Richard Capen, the president of the commission, rose in a hearing room filled with people and announced the verdict. "We, the Civil Service Commission of Los Angeles County, after hearing over one million words in over six weeks of testimony, find that not one charge against Dr. Thomas T. Noguchi has been proven. He is reinstated forthwith."

My fellow pathologists around the nation wired congratulations. They saw my survival as a victory for forensic science everywhere. But, even though I won my battle, those incredible charges were hard to live down, and sometimes I felt that strangers I met expected me to sprout wings and fly off into space, pausing only long enough to shoot down a 707.

It would take many years of serious scientific effort to rebuild my reputation. But in 1969 I was happy just to be back in my office in the job I loved. Then, only eight days after the verdict that had reinstated me, Los Angeles was struck by a tragedy that sent shivers throughout the world, and I found myself standing amidst the carnage of a mass murder which was the most brutal I had ever seen.

6

Medical Examiner's Case No. 69-8796

Sharon
Tate

A lonely road curved up a hill in Bel-Air until it reached an estate high on a cliff. An iron gate to the grounds was locked and the entire property fenced with barbed wire. Beyond the fence, a redwood house sat among trees on a spacious lawn, a swimming pool nestled beside it. A small guest house, behind the main residence, was the temporary home of the caretaker, nineteen-year-old William Garretson. Another young man, Steven Parent, who had been visiting Garretson, was about ready to leave. It was just after midnight, August 9, 1969.

Inside the main house a quiet social evening was winding down. Four princes and princesses of the Beverly Hills world were relaxing in the home rented by Sharon Tate and her husband, Polish movie director Roman Polanski. A tall, slender woman with brown hair, brown eyes and high cheekbones, Sharon Tate was considered one of Hollywood's most promising young actresses. In fact, the year before, in a poll of movie exhibitors taken by the *Motion Picture Herald,* she had been named a runner-up to Lynn Redgrave as the top "Star of Tomorrow." At twenty-six, she had already made ten films, and her future was luminous. But now she was happy for another reason. She was eight months pregnant. Her husband was in Europe working on a film, but she was looking forward to his return.

Abigail Folger was the heiress to the Folger coffee fortune. Her father would later tearfully describe "Gibby" as "a nice young girl from Radcliffe who suddenly found herself in that 'new world of Hollywood.' " The reason she was there was a tall, handsome man named Voyteck Frykowski, a friend of Roman Polanski and a prototypical member of what used to be called the Beautiful People. Vaguely wealthy, and definitely attractive to women, Frykowski raced sports cars, and had helped finance some of Polanski's films. Married twice, he was now romancing Abigail Folger, and both of them had been house guests of Sharon Tate for weeks.

Another "prince" there that night was one whom perhaps only Beverly Hills society would crown. A hairdresser who owned salons in Hollywood and elsewhere around the country, Jay Sebring was once engaged to Sharon Tate. He had become a friend of both Tate and her husband and was frequently a guest at their home. It would later be reported that part of Sebring's charm was that he was "kinky" in sex. He tied up women with a "small sash cord and then whipped them," which, if true, was apparently cheerfully accepted by all of his friends.

At midnight Sharon Tate was relaxing in bed, dressed only in a flowered bra and panties. Jay Sebring sat on the end of the bed chatting with her. Abigail Folger, in a white nightgown, had retired to the bedroom across the hall. She was reading a book. Voyteck Frykowski, her lover, had fallen asleep on a couch in the living room.

All was quiet at 10050 Cielo Drive.

A few minutes later, a car drove slowly up the dark road toward the secluded estate. A man, Tex Watson, and three girls, Susan Atkins, Patricia Krenwinkle and Linda Kasabian, were inside it. The girls were holding knives in their laps. The car stopped next to the gate, and Watson got out. He was carrying a long red-handled wire cutter. While the girls watched, he climbed up a metal pole and expertly cut the telephone wires to the house. Then he returned to the car and drove back down the road to park out of sight of the house.

It was approximately twelve-eighteen when they returned. The girls were barefoot, dressed in jeans and T-shirts. They carried dark clothes with them—and the long sharp knives they had been holding on their laps. They climbed over the fence and started toward the house. But trouble! Headlights! A car was approaching. "Get down. Get down," Watson whispered to the girls. They hurled themselves flat on the lawn and watched Watson walk toward the car, which had halted at the gate.

The next thing they heard was the voice of the young driver. "Please don't hurt me. I won't say anything."

Crack! A shot, then others. Steven Parent slumped over the wheel of his car, then toppled onto the passenger seat, dead.

Strangely, the shots were not heard by the people in the main residence, or by Garretson in the guest house beyond. The intruders waited tensely, expecting someone to emerge from the house to investigate. When no one did, they slipped on the dark garments which would make them all but invisible in the night. Then, holding the knives, the women padded barefoot, following Tex Watson with the gun, toward the pleasant redwood house with lighted windows.

Thirty minutes later there were unearthly screams —and turmoil as Frykowski and Folger tried to escape. Susan Atkins would later tell a cellmate that Sharon Tate had begged for her life. "I want to live. I want to have my baby."

Later that morning, police cars and ambulances lined the narrow road which led to the wooded estate. I made my way through the gate, where the LAPD homicide lieutenant in command greeted me. My staff assistants and paramedics were clustered around two bodies lying on the lawn in front of the house.

I was told that a third body had already been removed to our van because it had been found in a Rambler near the gate, within a few feet of where the press had gathered. A Rambler, I thought, among millionaires? What was the owner of such an inexpensive car doing in this area? I went to the van and checked the body. The young man had been shot in the head. "There's a caretaker, a kid named Garretson, alive," the lieutenant said. "He was in the guest house, and they missed him. He says the driver was visiting him."

The next body I checked was about twenty feet from the front door of the main residence. My investigator pulled back the sheet, and I saw a male Caucasian, in a purple shirt, open vest, and bell bottoms —all drenched in blood. I was told this was Voyteck Frykowski.

In my entire experience I had never seen such savagery applied to one person. Frykowski's face and head were crushed and bloodied by blows; his stomach, chest, limbs and back had been stabbed everywhere by knives; and there were bullet holes in his back. The autopsy would later reveal that he had been stabbed fifty-one times, clubbed with a blunt object thirteen times and shot twice.

I lifted his shirt and vest and studied the stab wounds. Because blood settles after the heart has stopped pumping, forensic pathologists can tell whether wounds were made before or after death. Postmortem wounds are lighter in color, and I counted several of those. It was quickly apparent that Frykowski had been stabbed repeatedly *after* he was dead or during the dying process. It was a pattern my staff and I would find repeated in all of the victims.

The next decedent was female, Caucasian, and pretty, with long hair in disarray. Abigail Folger lay on her back, dressed in a bloodied white nightgown, her arms outflung. She too had suffered multiple stab wounds both front and back.

Inside the house, I began to inspect the living room. There were pieces of a cracked gun butt near the door. Pools of blood were everywhere, and on the bottom of the front door a word had been scrawled in blood: "PIG."

"What do you think that means?" I asked the lieutenant.

"I don't know," he said. "The blacks call the cops 'pig'—but none of the victims were cops."

In the center of the room there was a sofa draped with a large American flag facing the fireplace. I walked around it and found two more bodies.

The male decedent was Jay Sebring, stylishly attired in white pants with blue longitudinal stripes, an open blue shirt, black boots and a wide belt. Like Frykowski, he had been both shot and stabbed in many places of his body. A bloody towel was wrapped around his head as a hood, and a rope was knotted around his throat.

The most pathetic victim, because she was obviously pregnant, was Sharon Tate, killed by multiple stab wounds. She was lying with her legs tucked up toward her stomach as if to protect her unborn child. And the rope tied to Sebring's throat was also wrapped around hers. It had been thrown over an exposed roof beam, apparently to hang the two victims.

I studied Sharon Tate's face closely and noted a rope burn on the lower part of her cheekbone. I then asked my investigator to examine the top of the beam around which the rope was looped. If the beam was deeply scratched or chipped, then we would know they had indeed been hanged.

The aide stood on the sofa to check and reported that there was only a slight abrasion, not a deep one, on the beam. That indicated to me that Tate and Sebring had been only partially suspended by their murderers, with their feet still on the floor.

I wondered why they had been "hanged" at all? "What does Homicide think happened here?" I asked the LAPD lieutenant.

"We think it's drug-connected, Dr. Noguchi," he said. "There's junk all over this place."

The police would later report that the following drugs had been found in and around the premises: thirty grams of hashish, along with ten capsules of MDA, a hypnotic drug, in the bedroom used by Frykowski and Folger; a gram of cocaine, six grams of marijuana and a partially smoked marijuana cigarette, all in Sebring's car; 6.9 grams of marijuana in a plastic bag in a cabinet in the living room; marijuana residue in the ashtray on the night table next to Sharon Tate's bed.

A drug-connected killing usually meant that its victims had reneged on a payment, and either a fight had broken out with the pushers or revenge had been taken. Drugs might also explain the excessive violence —killers stoned out of their minds, slashing their victims wildly. Criminals heavily into drug traffic were often black, and "pig," a word they might have used, had been scrawled in blood on the front door of the house.

The drug connection would remain the LAPD's main theory for weeks. And, in following it, they would ask me to withhold temporarily from the press the information that narcotics had been found on the premises. They had leads on two drug dealers and asked for my cooperation. I would give it to them, but I didn't believe their theory, even from the first moment I inspected the scene of the crimes. That symbolic hanging bothered me, especially in the context of such bizarre killings. To me, the massacre in the Tate house looked like ritual murder.

I knew there was a religious cult in San Francisco that practiced voodoo ceremonies, including the blood sacrifice of animals. We had been warned recently that the cult was establishing chapters in Los Angeles. But there were no animal sacrifices present here. Searching for another explanation, my eye fell on the large American flag draped over the couch. Could the murders be the work of a right-wing superpatriotic group? That theory also proved untenable when the housekeeper told me, "That flag has always been here. It came with the house."

When my investigation of the scene was complete, my aides started readying the bodies for transport to the morgue, placing paper bags over the hands so that any hair or skin caught under the nails in a struggle would be saved. Then they were wheeled out on stretcher carts to the waiting vans.

The sun was shining brightly that morning as the macabre parade of stretchers began. I paused for a moment before I followed them. To the right of where I stood, a cliff fell away hundreds of feet, and, below and beyond, the city of Los Angeles stretched to the horizon. It was my jurisdiction, I thought; my job to probe the underworld of terror and violence beneath the veneer of that city. But I had rarely faced brutality such as this.

Out by the fence, reporters were straining at a barricade manned by police. They waved note pads while television microphones and cameras poked over their shoulders. "Dr. Noguchi, Dr. Noguchi, what went on in there?" "Was it a sex party?" "How did they die?"

I shook my head. "No comment."

I was driven in our official car through the crowd of reporters and down the curving road up which the killers must have come the night before. After turning left on Sunset and driving through Beverly Hills into Hollywood, I saw the "flower children" who, in 1969, had taken over that section of the boulevard and transformed it into a hippie highway. Long hair, beards, jeans, sandals, boots, chains, bandanas, T-shirts, guitars and backpacks—hippies with beatific smiles, holding signs of love, and pounding angrily on a car if it didn't pick them up when they were hitchhiking. Their songs lyricized love for all mankind, in endless variations, but there was a violent undercurrent in the music, too.

However, most of the violence I had witnessed had occurred among the hippies themselves, not in the outside world. To them that world, filled with "straights," didn't even exist except as an object of derision. They had dropped out, creating their own society in communes in the countryside and in special sections in cities, such as Haight-Ashbury in San Francisco, and central Hollywood, through which Sunset Boulevard ran. They rarely ventured outside those areas. And that was why no one in the LAPD, nor I, as yet suspected hippies in the Tate killings. It wasn't their pattern to invade wealthy residential areas, either to steal or to kill.

When we stopped at a red light on the boulevard, two long-haired sixteen-year-old girls in cut-off jeans looked into the front of the car. "Hey," one said, "there's the Japanese coroner."

"Mr. Ghoul," the other one said. "Who are you burying today?"

Behind them I saw a boy sitting on the curb, his back against a lamppost, singing and strumming a guitar. I remember the words to this day. "It takes a worried man to sing a worried song. . . . It takes a worried man to sing a worried song."

Then we were off, turning onto the freeway for the long ride downtown to our office beneath the Hall of Justice. And there, as I remembered the scene of horror I had just left, I was indeed a worried man. The police theory of a drug-connected crime indicated that the orgy of murder in the Tate house would be a single event, not to be repeated. My theory of a ritual murder meant that the killers might be on the prowl again for new victims.

Leno and Rosemary La Bianca were "straights"— as different from hippies as they were from the Tate victims. La Bianca was a businessman, the president of a supermarket chain. His wife was the owner of a ladies' dress shop. They lived in the Los Feliz section of Los Angeles, an area of solid upper-middle-class working citizens.

The car that approached their house about 1 A.M. on August 10, 1969, was crowded with young killers. The four who had burst into the Tate estate were now joined by Leslie Van Houten—and by Charles Manson.

Manson was not at that time the bearded figure of evil who later became familiar to millions of Americans. He was clean-shaven, small and wiry. He slipped out of the car, holding a gun, and disappeared into the darkness toward the La Bianca house. Less than thirty minutes later he was back. "They're ready," he said.

"What happened?"

"A husband and wife are in there. I tied them up and told them, 'Don't worry. We don't intend to hurt you.' "

Tex Watson, Patricia Krenwinkle and Leslie Van Houten left the car and walked quietly toward the La Bianca house, where a frightened businessman and his wife had been promised that no one would hurt them.

At 11 A.M. the next day, I was performing the autopsy on Sharon Tate, while two of my associates autopsied the other victims. I studied the sixteen stab wounds in Tate's body with special care because I had been told by police that the knives employed in the orgy of murder had been taken away by the killers so that they could not be connected to the crime. But the murderers didn't know that an accurate description of those knives could be created by forensic science.

By techniques of wound analysis, forensic scientists can discover not only the measurements of a knife but its precise shape. Further, we can tell whether it is single- or double-edged, whether its tip is pointed or curved and whether its blade is grooved like a hunting knife.

I first measured the entrance of one of the wounds in Tate's body, which gave me the width and breadth of the blade. Then I looked for bruises on the surface of the skin at the point of entry. Such bruises would indicate that the handle of the knife had struck the body when the victim was stabbed, which meant that the entire blade had entered the wound. Therefore, in those wounds with bruises on the surface, I could discover the actual length of the knife by the depth of the wound.

The next step was to squeeze barium-sulfate paste into each wound until it filled the crevice. Then I made X-ray photographs of them, which, in conjunction with a close examination of the wounds, would enable me to tell police not only the exact dimensions of the knife that had killed Sharon Tate, but the interesting added information that it was double-edged, with a pointed tip.

Later, in court, that forensic evidence would prove to be important, because the murder weapon was never found. Linda Kasabian, who turned state's evidence, described it from memory, recalling that the length of the blade was between five and a half and six and a half inches. My autopsy showed that the knife was five inches long. She also testified that the width was about one inch; my report stated from one to one and a half inches. The thickness also matched. And then came the clincher. Kasabian testified that the knife had been sharpened on both sides and had a pointed tip, the exact knife I had described.

In sum, the weapon that had killed Sharon Tate and a second knife used in the murders, which was identified by the same process, were established to the satisfaction of the jury, even though the killers thought they had disposed of them.

During my autopsy, I also discovered that bones

had been struck by some of the knife thrusts into the bodies of the victims. At the trial, Kasabian testified that Patricia Krenwinkle had told her at the time of the murders that her hand ached from her knife striking bones. Thus another autopsy finding substantiated the verbal evidence of the state's witness.

But all that was in the future. On the morning of August 11, still completely mystified by the killings, I again noted the abrasion on Tate's cheek and pondered the enigma of the semihanging. At that moment an aide approached me, interrupting the autopsy. "Dr. Noguchi, a telephone call from Homicide. They say it's urgent."

"Urgent?"

I picked up the telephone and discovered that what I had feared earlier had come true. The killers had struck again—and once more there were symbols of a ritual murder.

Leno La Bianca was found lying on his back between a couch and a chair, dead from twenty-six stab wounds. But he too had been symbolically hanged, with a bloody pillowcase used as a hood over his head. A cord knotted around his throat was attached to a large, heavy lamp, and his hands were tied behind his back with a leather thong. An ivory-handled carving fork had also been used to stab him, and it was left protruding from his stomach.

His wife, Rosemary La Bianca, lay on the bedroom floor in a short pink nightgown and a blue dress with white stripes. The nightgown and the dress had been shoved up over her head by her killers. Stab wounds punctured her back and buttocks. She too was hooded in a pillowcase, and she had been "hanged" with a wire attached to a lamp.

"WAR" had been carved on the woman's abdomen. On the walls of the living room were written in blood "DEATH TO PIGS" and "RISE." And in the kitchen, on the refrigerator door, were the words "HELTER SKELTER."

The connections between the Tate and La Bianca murders were unmistakable to me—and to the press as well, as soon as the details were known. Their headlines trumpeted that relationship and plunged all of suburban Los Angeles into panic. Sales of guns for home defense quadrupled, guard dogs were purchased, and human bodyguards were hired, as residents feared there were killers on the loose who were slaughtering not only show-business figures but ordinary people as well.

However, the Los Angeles Police Department did not believe there was any connection at all between the two crimes. Inspector K. J. McCauley told the press, "I don't see any connection between this murder and the other. They're too widely removed. I just don't see any tie-up."

And a sergeant told reporters, "There is a similarity, but whether it's the same suspect or a copycat we just don't know."

There were valid reasons for the LAPD disbelief in a connection:

1. There was no apparent link between the two sets of victims, who were completely different from each other, one from the glamorous movie world, the other from business.

2. Robbery had occurred in the La Bianca case (Rosemary's wallet with cash and credit cards) but not in the Tate case.

3. Police detectives were hot on the trail of suspected drug dealers in the Tate case, while the La Biancas used no drugs at all.

The La Bianca killings *were* different in many crucial ways from the Tate murders. But to me the symbolic hangings and the words scrawled in blood at the scene of both crimes seemed to provide a significant, if puzzling, connection. The word "PIG" at the Tate house might have been written by a black drug dealer, as the LAPD believed. But at the La Biancas' the killers had also scrawled "RISE" and "HELTER SKELTER." What did those words have to do with drugs? Rather, they seemed to suggest the hand of a terrorist or revolutionary group.

For advice, I turned to Dr. Frederick Hacker, the psychiatrist who had recently testified in my defense before the Civil Service Commission, and who was one of the world's leading authorities on terrorism, its roots and its rites. He had published many articles and books on the subject and had been employed as a consultant in the terrorism field by both government and private sectors. It occurred to me that an expert such as Dr. Hacker, from his vast experience with terrorist groups, might discover an insight into these strange and violent murders.

I called Dr. Hacker to my office and told him it appeared that there was a common thread to the Tate and La Bianca killings. He was immediately fascinated, and I said I would give him copies of all the evidence and documentation I had, from the autopsy reports to the investigators' findings at the scenes of both murders. At my request, he readily agreed to volunteer as a consultant on these cases as a public service.

In our conversation we touched on several facts that seemed significant—in particular, the use of a wire cutter to snip the telephone lines to the Tate house, which indicated planning and that the victims weren't killed in a spontaneous frenzy. The rope over the beam and the towel on Sebring's head also intrigued Hacker, as did the word "PIG" on the door.

Ten days later he filed his report, and it was a stunner. Dr. Hacker, from his distinctive experience, saw a possible connection between the two crimes much more sinister than anyone could have imagined. These are some excerpts from his report:

It must be assumed that the [actual perpetrator's] helpers . . . were in a state of mind compatible with planning and at least a limited amount of anticipation of difficulties and premeditation (see cutting of wires, complicated rope arrangement, . . . keeping the victims controlled while the slaying went on, etc.) . . .

The bizarre features of the multiple crime certainly suggest severe psychopathology of the killers . . . (the possibility that an interested party might have hired impulsively sadistic killers cannot be excluded).

It is conceivable that the personality of the actual killer was quite different from those of his helpers and that . . . one party . . . carried out the preparations and precautionary measures while the other party or parties actually perpetrated the crimes. . . .

Thus, weeks before Charles Manson was found, Dr. Hacker predicated the existence of a man not even present at the scenes of the crimes, who had sent his "impulsively sadistic killers" to do his murdering. Hacker's report also went on to say that "the criminals might be looked for among fringe pseudo-religious groups"—a prophetic description of the cult of which Manson was the pseudogod.

Finally, in what I considered to be one of his most brilliant insights, Dr. Hacker said that the criminals might be a group of former associates of the victims who believed themselves "rejected, thwarted, cheated by one or more of the victims and who took revenge in this fashion."

Manson and his followers were eventually tried for the brutal slayings in Bel-Air and Los Feliz. Vincent Bugliosi, an extremely capable deputy district attorney, and his superior, Aaron Stovitz, head of the trials division, prosecuted the case against them. Bugliosi placed a cot in his office, working around the clock for months to secure their conviction. And one motive he ascribed to Manson was based on the words "Helter Skelter." In Bugliosi's statement at the trial,

The evidence will show that one of Manson's principal motives for these seven savage murders was to ignite Helter Skelter; in other words, start the black-white revolution by making it look as though the black man had murdered these seven Caucasian victims. In his twisted mind he thought this would . . . ultimately [lead] to a civil war between blacks and whites. . . . Manson envisioned that black people, once they destroyed the entire white race, would be unable to handle the reins of power because of inexperience and would therefore have to turn over those reins to those white people who had escaped from Helter Skelter— i.e. Charles Manson and his Family.

But another motive advanced by Bugliosi is one which my own research has led me to conclude is correct. Why did Manson choose Sharon Tate's residence for the orgy of murder? I believe that the pseudogod chose that particular house for a very mortal reason: symbolic revenge for a failed musical career. And after he had turned his worshiping cultists loose on Sharon Tate and her friends, the La Bianca murders were purely random, committed only to throw police off the real "revenge" trail at 10050 Cielo Drive.

Among the reports that crossed my desk as I was investigating the case, I found an odd fact that seemed to corroborate a motive of revenge. August 9, 1969, the date of the Tate massacre, was the exact anniversary of the day, one year before, when Manson made his first and only real step up the ladder as a rock-music singer. On that day he appeared at a studio in Van Nuys and recorded songs on tape, at the behest of a talent scout, Gregg Jakobsen.

Things must have looked bright for Manson that morning. Dennis Wilson of the Beach Boys had not only befriended him but had allowed Manson and some of his followers to live in his mansion on Sunset Boulevard and hobnob with movie stars at parties. Even better, Terry Melcher, the son of Doris Day, had "promised" to produce a record album starring Charles Manson.

Terry Melcher lived at 10050 Cielo Drive.

But after the recording session, Melcher, according to Manson and his followers, reneged on his "promise." Melcher has always said that it was all a misunderstanding. He made no such commitment. But, whatever happened, Manson's musical "career" began to collapse right there. A year later, down and out in a dirty commune on a shabby "ranch," the glory days of Hollywood and fame as a rock singer denied him forever, he decided to strike back at the Hollywood society that had coldly rejected him. And I believe he chose not only a special anniversary day for his revenge, but also a special house: 10050 Cielo Drive, where his "sponsor" and symbol of his betrayal, Terry Melcher, had lived, and where Manson had visited.

At his trial, Tex Watson testified, "Manson told me to take the gun and knife and go up to where Terry Melcher used to live. He said to kill everybody in the house as gruesome as I could." And by "gruesome," Watson said, Manson meant that "witchery" should be included. That was why their orgy of killing included the strange "hanging" of Tate and Sebring and the bloody message scrawled on the door.

Thus, neither Manson's choice of day nor his choice of house was coincidental. The tragic coincidence was that Sharon Tate, lovely and pregnant, and three of her friends were in the house that night. They died with barefoot, lank-haired young girls brutally thrusting knives into their bodies, girls programmed by a "god" who, I believe, was more mortal than they knew. He craved success on earth.

7

Medical Examiner's Case No. 70-10463

Janis Joplin

Barney's Beanery was a famous late-night restaurant in Hollywood. The menu was modest, the prices were cheap, and the ambience was almost always electric with the presence of celebrated Hollywood stars.

Janis Joplin and band member Ken Pearson were at the bar on the night of October 4, 1970. Joplin was sipping vodka and orange juice. The two of them had just returned from a Hollywood recording studio, where they had listened to tapes which were to be included in Joplin's new album, "Pearl."

Shortly after midnight, Pearson drove Joplin to the Landmark Hotel in Hollywood, where the band was staying. Joplin told him she was enthusiastic about the new album. In fact, all evening she had been in a cheerful mood. Pearson didn't know that one reason for her high spirits was that at four o'clock that afternoon Joplin had been visited by her drug connection. Now the two of them went to their separate rooms. Joplin's was on the first floor. Less than half an hour later she emerged from her room and reentered the lobby, where she told a clerk she needed change for a five-dollar bill to buy some cigarettes.

The clerk would later tell police that she spoke casually to him and seemed perfectly natural. In fact, it's not known definitely at what time that night Janis Joplin plunged a needle into her arm, injecting a lethal dose of heroin into her blood. Sometimes there is a delay in the reaction, and it's medically possible, but unlikely, that she had already injected herself before the visit to the lobby and the informal chat with the clerk. But when the time came, the heroin took savage effect and Joplin crumpled to the floor beside her bed, her body, clad in a nightgown, wedged against a bedside table.

Three weeks earlier a male rock star, Jimi Hendrix, had OD'd in a London apartment. And the deaths of these two stars, one following so closely after the other, stunned their legion of fans. A *New York Times* writer began his article on Joplin: "God, what a year this is turning out to be. . . . the king and the queen of the gloriously self-expressive music that came surging out of the late sixties are dead, the victims, directly or indirectly, of the very real physical excesses that were part of the world that surrounded them."

The "Queen of Rock," now a drug victim, was born in Port Arthur, Texas, where, she later said, she was a "misfit." "I read, I painted. I didn't hate niggers. Man, those people back home hurt me."

From the first she loved music, collecting Bessie Smith records and singing at charity functions around town. But she had never sung professionally at all when she received a telephone call from a friend, Travis Rivers, in San Francisco. He had formed a band called Big Brother and the Holding Company. Janis Joplin joined the group in Haight-Ashbury, and a legend was born.

From the start her animal vitality dominated her audiences. Foot-stomping, arm-waving, gyrating her hips, she energized her young listeners and sent them into a frenzy. As she told a Reuters reporter later, "I couldn't believe it, all that rhythm and power. I got stoned just feeling it, like it was the best dope in the world. It was so sensual, so vibrant, loud, crazy. I couldn't stay still; I had never danced when I sang, but there I was moving and jumping. I couldn't help myself, so I sang louder and louder. By the end I was wild."

Somewhere along the way Joplin was introduced to hard drugs and became a user. According to her friends, at the time of her death she was fighting the habit, and had actually stayed off drugs for weeks before beginning the injections again.

What would cause a later controversy was the fact that Joplin had not injected a great amount of heroin into her veins that night. Indeed, at an insurance trial in 1974 related to her death it was stated that the amount of heroin was not overwhelmingly large. Why, then, did Janis Joplin die?

I supervised Janis Joplin's autopsy, where evidence of multiple old punctures was found in the veins of her arms. When a needle is injected into a vein it causes a minute injury, and after it has healed a tiny, almost microscopic indentation can be observed in the vein. There were many of those—and one fresh puncture which had not healed.

We sent Joplin's blood to the toxicological laboratory to be tested for drugs, which we believed were almost certainly the cause of her death. And since there was no evidence that anyone had been with her either shortly before or at the time of her death, we also believed that the lethal drugs had been self-injected. But then we received word that no drugs had been found in her room. Thus there arose the possibility of an accomplice in Joplin's death. And was it the result of an accidental overdose or murder?

I decided to go to Joplin's hotel room, where an LAPD policeman was on duty when I arrived. He told me that a needle and syringe had been recovered from the scene, but no heroin.

I made my customary survey of the room and looked into a wastepaper basket. It contained a red "balloon" with heroin. "What's this?" I asked the policeman.

He came over and stared. "Hey, where'd that come from?" The expression on his face was comical. "We went over this room a hundred times and that basket was empty."

"Have there been any visitors to the room?" I asked.

The policeman said that a fellow band member (or her manager, I have forgotten the associate he named) had stopped around to check her personal effects.

I smiled. "He may have removed the drug after her

death and then realized it was evidence. So he came back and dropped it in the wastepaper basket." It was not an unusual occurrence in drug cases. Often, the first reaction of friends is to remove the evidence of drug use. But they usually return with it when they have thought things over.

I took the "balloon" back to our toxicology laboratory for testing to make certain the substance it contained was heroin. Meanwhile, the results of the lab tests had arrived on my desk, showing that Joplin had morphine in her blood. (Heroin breaks down into morphine in the system.) But judging from the amount of heroin left in the package, it did not appear that Joplin had injected herself with a very large dose. No doubt she had taken a similar dose hundreds of times before with no side effects. But now, suddenly, she had died from a "normal" dose. Why?

The answer to that question is the essence of the danger of street drugs. You never know what you are getting. Heroin is cut in many ways. On the East Coast it's often adulterated with lactose or quinine. On the West Coast, the dealers most often cut it with procaine (an anesthetic drug) or PCP (a violence-producing drug), Vitamin C or Insitol (lactose sugar). But perhaps the most dangerous adulterant is talcum powder, which is asbestos and ends up in the lungs.

Ironically, the reason for Janis Joplin's death was exactly the opposite of the many tragedies caused by cut heroin. When an analysis of the contents of the "balloon" came back from the lab, I found that what the dealer had sold Joplin was almost pure heroin, so pure that it had more than ten times the power of the normal heroin she used. Cut drugs are generally one to three percent heroin; the drug Janis Joplin had used was forty to fifty percent heroin. Her system was not prepared for, and could not cope with, the unexpected jolt.

Janis Joplin's death highlighted once again the dangers of drug abuse. As a medical examiner I have all too often seen its disastrous consequences, and in an attempt to deal with the problem my colleagues and I urged the California legislature to pass a bill which would require that all deceased drivers be tested not only for alcohol but for drugs, thus providing medical examiners with another statistical tool to help identify trends in drug use so that we can better deal with them.

Such trends had been monitored by our office and others around the nation for years. Heroin use, ironically, dropped off in the very year Janis Joplin died—and I believe that the shock of her death may have had something to do with that phenomenon. But today there's a new danger. The drug of choice is cocaine, which, unlike heroin, is not so devastating and overwhelming that the user can hardly function. In fact, it is a stimulant, whereas heroin is a downer. Nevertheless, cocaine is a risky drug. At least fifteen deaths a year in Los Angeles are a direct result of sniffing or injection, while countless other deaths are related to its use. And the human toll cannot be measured: the deterioration of the brain through habitual stimulation, the damage to the nervous system, the dependency on the drug which causes addicts to steal and even murder to acquire the money for the expensive habit.

Another drug, which has not gained as much publicity, may be the most dangerous of all. PCP, sometimes used to cut heroin, is also widely used by members of the below-poverty community, and it's a frightening drug indeed, because it directly stimulates violence. Some time ago I noted more and more PCP addicts among decedents in Los Angeles, and I identified its use as a trend which is still not widely recognized in this country, but which I believe will cause much trouble and tragedy ahead.

It was ironic that Janis Joplin died in the Landmark Hotel, for she too was a landmark in the history of rock, a talented young woman who left behind a powerful message in her music and in the tragic circumstances of her death.

8

Mass Disasters

Surely, of all of the states of the Union, California is among the leaders in mass disasters. Indeed, predictions are constantly being made both by prophets of doom and by distinguished scientists that California will one day slide completely into the ocean, disappearing beneath the sea forever, and that the famous San Andreas Fault will be the breaking point from which the state takes leave of the continent.

There *is* a San Andreas Fault, and there certainly are earthquakes in California. In addition, the state is annually beset not only by ocean storms that batter its beaches, but by forest fires that rage out of control, avalanches that careen through villages, and mudslides that carry away highways and homes. Regrettably, all of these natural disasters cause loss of lives. So it is necessary for any California medical examiner to set up a plan of operation to deal with them.

Very early in my career as Chief Medical Examiner I established such an emergency plan in which, as soon as word of a mass disaster was received, various special teams would go into action. Among those teams were the investigators who would be sent to the scene of the disaster as quickly as possible; the forensic pathologists who would direct the medical and legal investigation; the toxicologists and criminalists who would find forensic clues; the forensic odontologists and anthropologists who would help identify the bodies of the victims; the identification and notification personnel who would inform local police in cities where the victims lived and would call surviving family members for information which would help identify the bodies; and the liaison team which would help coordinate our efforts with the FBI, the LAPD, the Sheriff's Office, the LA Fire Department and various other government agencies.

I called the mass-disaster investigators my Go Team, men and women who, in addition to their forensic specialties, were trained in physical fitness by the Sheriff's Office, for often their jobs entailed considerable risk. And they were prepared to respond not only to natural disasters but also to man-made disasters, including multiple murders, fires, and airplane crashes.

Such a call came in on June 6, 1971. One of America's worst air tragedies had occurred.

Hughes Air West Jetliner Flight 706, carrying forty-three passengers and a five-man crew, departed from

Los Angeles International Airport at 5:50 P.M. that day, heading east. At the same time, a Navy F-4 Phantom jet with a crew of two and faulty radar hurtled through the sky on a collision course. Below it, twenty miles east of metropolitan Los Angeles, were the San Gabriel Mountains, a range of sharp peaks and densely forested gorges often described as one of the most rugged areas in America.

At twelve thousand feet, the Navy jet plowed directly into the commercial airliner. A fiery explosion erupted in the sky, incinerating many passengers in their seats. Then the airliner disintegrated into small pieces, and bodies tumbled through the air. So total was the disintegration of the airliner that no sizable fragment was ever found. The bodies and dismembered parts of the victims were strewn for miles in the mountains.

Our office was notified at once, and within minutes I ordered our mass-disaster teams to report for duty. The bodies of the victims would have to be identified for both medical and legal reasons, including insurance purposes, and for the sake of their relatives.

"How do we get to the site of the crash?" I asked.

"There are no roads," I was told. "The nearest town is miles away, so we'll have to drop your men in by helicopter."

Clad in our Go Team uniforms—red hard hats, boots, and khaki overalls with "CORONER" in gold letters on the back—an advance team of investigators and I were flown toward the disaster area. But even before we arrived, I knew there would be trouble, not only from the forbidding terrain but from a dense fog which was rolling in and obscuring the mountains.

The advance team's job was to work with other Go Teams from the Sheriff's Office and the LA County Fire Department to clear an area in the mountain forest for a helicopter pad, set up a communication station and begin the search for bodies. Its members were supplied with tools and other equipment and also with a canvas tent and enough food to last for a week. And a week's time might be necessary, I thought. I had already been informed of the dimensions of our task: bodies separated by miles in the rugged terrain and most likely burned beyond recognition.

As we approached the scene through the fog, we could see helicopters dispatched by fire authorities hovering over a gorge. But when our own helicopter dipped low, we could barely discern fire and rescue personnel moving like ghosts in a shroud of fog in the underbrush. The advance team quickly assembled its equipment and descended by rope ladder to the ground. We lowered the rest of their supplies to them, but even as we hovered right above them they began to disappear in the underbrush and the thickening fog.

I knew that no search for bodies would be possible that night, but the team could begin work on the clearing and set up a radio communications station. I did not envy them their job. But I knew they were well trained and well equipped—with one possible exception. As we were about to leave them on the mountain all night, one of the members of the team had a last-minute request: "Dr. Noguchi, at least drop us a six-pack of beer!"

When I returned the next morning, our advance team and a similar disaster team from the Sheriff's Office called the Mountain Goats had worked all night, clearing away trees and underbrush to create a helicopter pad and set up a radio communications station. Other members of the Go Team were landed in the area, while I hovered above it in a helicopter, maintaining close radio communication to coordinate our search in conjunction with the helicopters from the fire and rescue authorities. For it was immediately apparent that a ground reconnaissance would be futile; the scrub grass was five feet tall, obscuring everything.

Instead, the search would have to be accomplished from the air. The helicopters flew low until someone spotted a body or a dismembered part. Then they hovered over the site, and the wind from the rotor blades blew the underbrush aside so that the obscured body could be seen. Its location was radioed to our Go Team members on the ground, and they made their way through the dense underbrush to the body.

But it was dangerous work for the helicopters, hovering so closely to the ground in mountainous territory. The whirling rotor blade of one helicopter struck an exposed boulder on a slope, and the copter crashed but did not explode. We quickly rescued the shaken and slightly injured pilot, brought him up into another helicopter and flew him to the medical station.

The difficult search went on for the next several days. The members of the Go Team labeled each body they found "Doe One," "Doe Two," "Doe Three," etc.—not John or Jane Doe, because most of the charred remains could not be immediately identified as male or female. They also searched nearby for articles which might help identify the victim and placed them in a bag with the same "Doe" label as the body. And they were alert for any items that might concern national security as well as property of special significance. (Once in a helicopter crash a few years before, a representative of an auto manufacturer had been carrying the top-secret advance design for the company's newest model. We retrieved the design on the ground and returned it to the company safely, with its secrecy unbreached.)

Eventually, each body found on the ground from the Hughes Airlines crash was wrapped and placed in a helicopter for transport to an emergency staging area. Dismembered parts of bodies were also placed in bags and brought to the staging area, a high-school playground in the city of Duarte, where huge tents had been erected to house the rescue teams and the sheriff's deputies and to receive the bodies.

When all the victims of the crash had been assembled at the staging area, they were transferred to the Medical Examiner's Office in Los Angeles, where the process of identification could begin. Any stranger who had seen the bodies in the staging area might have said that such identification would be impossible. Almost all of them were totally charred, with no fingerprints. But we set out to do it by what could be called simple deduction, or what computer engineers call, more technically, "the branching technique."

To begin with, all the dismembered bodies were made whole—that is, arms and legs reassembled. When bone and tissue are torn, the tear leaves a unique pattern which can be used to match body parts. There were forty whole victims, but because of the burning none of them could be visually identified by relatives, and only one or two had discernible fingerprints.

To establish their identity, we made a huge chart to match information. From the passenger manifesto we listed the names and addresses of the victims. Each was classified by sex and approximate age; the presence of arthritis or an enlarged prostate gland, for example, indicated an older person. And then, under the direction of Dr. Dean V. Wiseley, chief of the forensic-medicine division, deputy medical examiners performed autopsies with a special mission: to discover any unique feature of every body. Was there an old fracture? A hysterectomy or an appendectomy? A still-visible scar? If so, this information was placed on the chart under the appropriate "Doe" labels.

Meanwhile, our identification and notification team was telephoning relatives for information about each of the victims. Among other questions, they asked for the precise height, the color of eyes and hair (the hair roots sometimes survive fire), the surgical history, and the presence of unique scars or body characteristics.

As this process was going on, the deputy dental examiner was at work obtaining the victims' dental charts from all over the United States. And the forensic anthropologists in our office were separating the victims' bodies by race.

Once all this information had been assembled, we could match it to the information we had discovered through autopsies and X rays of the entire body of each victim. Surgical histories were particularly useful in identifying the victims. In some cases, surgical pins associated with an operation were still in the body, and those pins often contained serial numbers relating to a patient. Depending on the model, we could tell where the manufacturer was located, and sometimes even the area where the surgery had been performed.

To establish the color of the hair and eyes of each victim, we sometimes placed roots of hair from the scalp or the armpit that had survived the fire under the microscope. Melanin is a brown pigment which gives color to hair. Lighter amounts of the chemical cause blond hair and blue eyes, larger amounts dark hair and brown eyes. Matching the color of hair and eyes with the information obtained from relatives of the victims provided two more clues in the identification procedure.

Artifacts found on the body or nearby, such as rings or unburned ID papers, also helped in the massive identification effort. And false teeth. Dental laboratories often place the doctor's name and the date of manufacture on their dentures. Thus we could find out the name of the wearer, a process that would be even easier if, as I had suggested many times to dental associates, the wearer's Social Security number was also stamped on the dentures. (In 1983, such a law was passed in California.)

In the end every victim of the San Gabriel tragedy was identified. Our mass-disaster teams—from the advance investigators to the notification and identification personnel—performed so efficiently and expeditiously that our office gained a worldwide reputation for our work, with the result that years later, when a Pan American airliner crashed on the Pacific island of Pago Pago thousands of miles away, killing 102 people, all of the bodies that were burned beyond recognition were flown to our forensic center in Los

Angeles, by request of the Federal Aviation Administration, for identification.

That was an even more difficult job than the San Gabriel disaster. One third of the passengers were Samoans, there were a few Taiwanese and other Orientals, and the rest were Caucasians. And the initial job of differentiating between the Caucasian and Oriental victims fell largely to the forensic anthropologists in our office, working with the following skeletal characteristics of both races:

1. Almost all Orientals have high cheekbones.

2. The dimensions of the heads from front to back and from right to left are rounder in Orientals than in Caucasians. The typical Caucasian skull is longer from front to back than from right to left. It is also longer vertically than the typical Oriental skull.

3. Most Orientals have shovel-shaped incisor teeth.

4. The opening for the nose in most Oriental skulls is different because the nose is shorter and wider than the typical Caucasian nose.

To differentiate the Samoan victims of the crash from the Taiwanese, we relied on one anthropological fact. Polynesian Orientals, such as Samoans, tend to have heavier bones because they are, in general, a more muscular people. And to support those muscles, their bones are substantially stronger and larger than those of other Orientals.

Once racial classifications had been made, we used the same forensic techniques to identify the victims that had proved so effective in the San Gabriel disaster. But dental and fingerprint records were almost nonexistent for the Samoan victims, and when our investigators telephoned Samoans for information about their relatives their replies were often too vague to be helpful. To the question "How tall was your brother?" would come over the telephone the answer "As high as *this*," with no further amplification.

Eventually, however, we were able to identify every single victim of the crash, adding to the reputation of the work our office could do in mass disasters. It was one of the ironies of my career as Chief Medical Examiner that, in 1969, I had been accused of "praying" for such disasters. Unfortunately, they occurred —with no "divine" intervention from me. My prayer was only that the Medical Examiner's Office would always be prepared to meet these tragic emergencies.

9

A Passion
for Science

"Good morning, ladies and gentlemen. It is indeed my pleasure to welcome the medical examiners, members of law enforcement agencies, scientists and designers of forensic instruments to this, our first seminar on death investigation."

On May 22, 1972, I stood in the sunlight in front of a gleaming new four-story building on Mission Street —the Los Angeles County Forensic Science Center. To celebrate its opening, hundreds of experts in forensic science and law enforcement had come to the center from all over the country to participate in our first seminar, which would last for three days and climax with the ceremonies dedicating the building.

I had fought hard for the new center, but I was by no means solely responsible for its construction. My predecessor, Dr. Curphey, had first envisioned such a forensic center and worked tirelessly to bring it into being, as had every forensic scientist compelled for years to work in overcrowded, ill-equipped quarters in the Hall of Justice. My outspoken demands on behalf of the center had been, in 1969, among the reasons given for my dismissal, and once I was reinstated I pursued the same goal somewhat more diplomatically, if no less insistently. But in the end it was no single voice that led to the construction of the center. Rather, it was the sheer volume of work the Medical Examiner's Office had to perform in such a sprawling and populous metropolitan area, and the growing complexity of forensic science itself. Both necessitated more space, a larger staff, and the latest in technological equipment. Modern medical facilities are a far cry from the hospitals of only a few years ago. Forensic centers, too, once little more than morgues, were forced to change and grow with the times.

The new building also represented the realization of a new approach to forensic science: the "total investigation" of a case. When I first joined the Los Angeles Medical Examiner's staff, we didn't even employ investigators. Deputy coroners merely picked up bodies after the police had conducted their investigations, then performed medical autopsies and associated laboratory testing—and relied on the LAPD, the Sheriff's Office and other law enforcement agencies for all other necessary evidence surrounding the deaths.

That had changed, thanks in part to my own efforts as well as those of other forensic scientists who shared the same vision of the total-investigation approach. Well before the construction of the new building, the

Medical Examiner's Office began to employ investigators to go to the scene of a death, collect evidence and interview witnesses. Autopsies had become medical-legal forensic investigations, including, if necessary, a reenactment of the episode of death and the careful analysis of laboratory results to determine its cause. We also prepared for trial and testimony in court, if that too was necessary. And, finally, we sought means to prevent similar fatal incidents.

Modern technology had come to play an increasingly vital part in all those activities. Scientific techniques and equipment unknown to forensic scientists a decade before were now used as a matter of routine. In the new center, we would employ the most innovative computerized equipment to assist the scientists on our staff. And, continuing another trend in the total-investigation approach, we could reach beyond our staff into scores of other disciplines for expert consultants in cases on which they were needed.

By 1972, our office had already utilized more than one hundred fifty multidiscipline consultants in almost every field imaginable to aid us in our work. And I was a leading proponent of the use of one category of specialists in particular: behavioral scientists qualified to conduct "psychological autopsies." Stated most simply, if suicide was suspected as the cause of death, a psychological autopsy examined evidence of the victim's state of mind at the time, thus helping to confirm —or disprove—that suspicion. If homicide had occurred, the psychological autopsy focused on the perpetrator as well as the victim, examining evidence at the scene in an attempt to analyze the personality and motives of one who would commit such a crime. Psychological autopsies had begun as an idea of Dr. Curphey's in the uproar surrounding Marilyn Monroe's death. And since Dr. Frederick Hacker's report had proved literally prophetic in the Manson murders, I had made them a regular tool of our department in cases where they were appropriate.

After concluding my opening remarks on that bright May morning, I led a tour through the new Forensic Science Center, in which the total-investigation approach would be conducted. It began in the sub-basement of the 55,000-square-foot building where evidence and property were labeled and stored. Also located there were a storage room for supplies, the huge refrigeration power source and offices for the maintenance staff.

Almost all of our laboratory equipment was housed on the floors above, but perhaps the most ultramodern, sophisticated piece of equipment was installed in the sub-basement: the scanning electron microscope (SEM). Because the SEM was so sensitive that it had to be situated in an area with the least vibration, we housed it on this underground floor along with another sensitive device, the transmission electron microscope (TEM).

The TEM was an electronic version of that age-old tool of scientists, the microscope. In a conventional microscope, light waves pass through a specimen and a sequence of lenses to form a magnified image; this type of microscope can magnify any object up to twenty-five hundred times its normal size. In the TEM, electrons take the place of light waves, and electromagnetic lenses replace the glass lenses. Powerful indeed, the TEM can magnify more intensely than any other instrument—a virus in a single cancer cell, for example, and internal structures of the body such as blood cells. For that reason, it is a very useful device in determining natural causes of death, as well as detecting changes caused by drugs or poisons in cells.

But forensic scientists are often more interested in changes in the surfaces of tissue—minute, telltale evidence left by, for example, a bullet, a knife or a blunt object. The SEM employs different technology to accomplish this. Electrons scan back and forth across a specimen, and the image, with a magnification of up to fifty thousand times the size of the specimen, is projected onto a television screen, permitting the viewer to see its surface in three-dimensional detail. Used in conjunction with X-ray and fluorescent equipment, the SEM was a boon to forensic science because it could precisely identify microscopic bits of metallic elements in bullet-wound paths. It could also tell us whether a burn was caused by a cigarette, a fire or torture, and whether a cancer was caused by asbestos. There are four different kinds of asbestos crystals; the SEM could tell which asbestos was present.

The next stop on my tour was the security and service floor on the level above the sub-basement. Three autopsy rooms were located on that floor. Room A, the main autopsy room, contained six stainless-steel tables, each with the necessary appliances, such as a weighing scale and a sink with running water. The tables were deliberately placed close to each other so that medical examiners could confer, if necessary. Because of the noise from electric saws and other equipment, there was a soundproof booth in a corner of the room where forensic pathologists could dictate their notes.

Room B had only one autopsy table next to the X-ray-facilities area. That room was for cases where more meticulous study had to be done. Our staff called it the VIP Room. But actually it would be utilized for cases of special medical difficulty or significance.

Room C was a larger room specially designed for cases of infectious disease, or for bodies in advanced decomposition. It was airtight, with a special air-conditioning system which sucked infected gases from the body and transferred them to an incinerator on the roof, where they were destroyed by fire.

A large staging room, the investigation division, the color-photo-processing, photo-file and X-ray rooms, the forensic-dental offices and the neuropathology laboratory were also located on this level. It was the floor on which the bodies arrived at the center. The processing of a decedent began in the staging room, where the body was placed on a gurney and weighed on a huge scale. Meanwhile, a personal-effects inventory was taken. The investigator who had been to the scene of the death turned in a receipt for all evidence and personal property he had recovered there. The inventory had to be signed not only by our investigator but by a member of another agency, such as the LAPD.

Then our staff photographers, under the direction of the medical examiner in charge, carefully took photographs of the body, first fully clothed if that was its condition, and continuing as layer after layer of clothing was removed. Fingerprints were taken routinely, in case a homicide might be involved.

After being photographed, the body was stored in our huge walk-in refrigerator on the same floor, awaiting autopsy if appropriate. The victim's property was also stored.

Identification of the body was usually accomplished at the scene of death through witnesses, as well as through the personal effects of the victim. But if there was no such identification, relatives were asked to come to the center.

An autopsy, if necessary, generally took place the next day. When it was completed, the body was sutured and prepared for release to a funeral home. The body was embalmed, if the family wished, and this was done also in cases where the body had to be stored for long periods of time because of lack of identification.

The next stop on my tour was the public floor at ground level, where the lobby and the reception desk for visitors were located. Also on this floor were the offices of the chief deputy medical examiner and the chief of the forensic-medicine division, and a suite for resident pathologists who were sent from various hospitals on a rotating basis to be trained in forensic pathology.

Finally, this floor contained the clerical offices where the myriad details of a forensic-science center were handled, from coordinating subpoenas in court cases to entering all relevant data concerning each case into computers so that it could later be retrieved. The public has the right of access to information concerning medicolegal investigations.

A special feature of the new building, a closed-circuit-television room, was also located on this floor.

Formerly, bereaved relatives would have to view a body close up for identification—an emotionally wrenching experience. Now they could sit in this room upstairs and view the face of the victim on a television screen, thus aiding the process of identification with less pain to relatives and friends.

The second floor of the building was laboratory country, in particular the toxicology lab, which was equipped with the latest technology, including the basic device for analyzing chemicals in the blood, the gas chromatograph (GC) machine. In the days of Marilyn Monroe, blood analysis was done on a primitive piece of equipment called a UV spectrometer which analyzed blood in liquid form. An extract was exposed to ultraviolet rays to measure the types and amounts of the chemicals. Then the extract was absorbed in a vertical filter paper. The height of absorption determined the identity of the chemical in the blood. For example, among barbiturates, Seconal was the highest, Nembutal second and phenobarbital the lowest.

The GC machine provided a much more accurate analysis. In that device, blood heated in a tiny oven emitted gas which contained the various chemical elements in the blood. As each element of the gas moved up a column along with a flow of inert gas such as helium, the *speed* of its movement was measured. And because we know the precise speed with which each element moves, we can thus identify the element.

The GC machine recorded this information in the form of peaks on a graph. The distance between peaks showed the speed of movement, identifying the chemical element or drug in the blood. The height of the peak showed us the amount of the drug which was present.

Our laboratory had all types of GC machines for various special purposes. But by far the most sophisticated was the GC mass spectrometer connected to a computerized data system. The mass spectrometer utilized a technology different from that of the GC. It subjected the chemical elements in a gas to electron bombardment, which broke them down into molecules. A computer then measured the molecular weight of each molecule, comparing it with a library of data to determine the chemical in question. All chemicals have different molecular weights, so the chemical could be precisely identified. With the conventional GC, such identification was not always precise. The computerized GC mass spectrometer, on the other hand, was one hundred percent accurate.

Our laboratories were equipped with many different kinds of spectrometer, such as light, ultraviolet, infrared and atomic-absorption devices for special purposes, which included analyzing organic compounds that are not gaseous and detecting and identifying metallic elements.

In addition to the toxicology lab, elsewhere on the second floor were other labs specializing in histopathology, with equipment for analyzing tissue structure; in serology, equipped to analyze biological fluids such as semen in rape cases and blood and bloodstains for typing; in forensic biology, with equipment to analyze trace evidence such as broken glass, paints, soil, plankton in drowning cases, botanical materials and digested food; in odontology for bite-mark identification and matching of teeth; and in anthropology to study skeletons to determine age, sex and race. This floor also held the offices of the senior members of the staff, including my own. And there I demonstrated the closed-circuit color-television system through which I could monitor various functions in the building. I was especially proud of the system which used cameras suspended directly above the autopsy tables. Through it, a pathologist conducting an autopsy could communicate any questions (or surprises) directly to me and I could see what he was referring to. My pride was misplaced, however, and the system was later removed for a very practical reason: the pathologists kept bumping their heads on the cameras.

As time went on, we would find other "bugs" in the building. But I was certain that with its completely up-to-date facilities and equipment, not only could the Medical Examiner's Office better perform its mandated function, but my associates and I could also continue our experiments with new techniques, thus enlarging our knowledge of the causes of death.

The media, however, seemed frankly skeptical. On hand for dedication day, May 25, 1972, were Joseph Busch, the District Attorney of Los Angeles; Liston Witherill, director of the Department of Hospitals; Dr. Theodore J. Curphey, my ex-boss; and various members of the Los Angeles County Board of Supervisors, along with representatives of the press and television sent to cover the event. Some of the press appeared a bit shocked at this "monument to death" which had arisen, sphinxlike, in their city. In the weeks preceding the dedication, they had bombarded me with questions which revealed the public's lack of knowledge of the real mission of forensic science even as late as

1972. Was such a modern and expensive facility necessary? they asked. What were my plans to utilize it? Why so much sophisticated equipment?

If the tide of homicides and unexplained deaths kept rising in Los Angeles, I told them, an even larger building with *more* sophisticated equipment might someday be necessary to accomplish our duty under law, a statement that was to prove even more prophetic than I knew at the time. And I went on to explain some of the projects I had in mind to expand the scope of the Medical Examiner's Office and its contributions to the community.

Organ transplants can save lives, I told reporters, and I wanted to make certain that our office worked with physicians and hospital administrators to assist them in locating donor organs. (Eleven years later, in 1983, I would be invited to the wedding of Cynthia Jelkman, twenty-five, who had received a heart for organ transplant from the Forensic Science Center. We became acquainted, and one day I introduced her to a friend of mine, Wesley Parker, a master chef. He was the man she married.)

I also told reporters that the Medical Examiner's Office should be a watchdog for the quality of life in the community, aiding those who sought to curb the pollution of our environment. And because drugs and alcohol caused so many deaths, our office would work strongly on community programs to curb their abuse. Our office, I said, would address itself to the *prevention* of unexpected and unnecessary deaths by such drugs.

Many of those programs were already under way; others remained for the future. For example, I wanted our office to help establish guidelines, in conjunction with hospitals and physicians, in regard to the termination of life-support systems in cases of patients with irreversible brain damage. It wasn't until 1982, through joint committees of the Los Angeles County Medical and Bar Associations, that such guidelines were established. And in 1983, the joint committee began to address similar guidelines for cases of patients in a prolonged vegetative state.

Because Los Angeles is on the sea and ideal for underwater diving, I had long been active on underwater-safety committees. In the years ahead, our office would pioneer in the investigation of underwater deaths. I was also interested in the very young and the very old. I wanted our office to be in the forefront of efforts to curb child abuse and battered-children deaths, surely the most pathetic decedents to enter our facility. Years later, Los Angeles County established ICAN, the Interagency Council on Child Abuse and Neglect, to deal with this problem. The council included law enforcement and social-service agencies, together with the Medical Examiner's Office.

No less serious was the problem of abuse and neglect of the aged, and I believed we should investigate nursing-home deaths. At the time, the law forbade this, but some years later my colleagues and I succeeded in getting the law amended, and the Medical Examiner's Office now has the jurisdiction to investigate suspicious nursing-home deaths.

Thus I participated in the dedication day ceremonies with great pride in the new Forensic Science Center. But at the same time I was thinking of the future. Whatever the accomplishments of the Medical Examiner's Office in the past, there was still so much left to be done. For the life and work of any chief medical examiner are science and leading a scientifically motivated organization in the search for innovations and in the development of new technology that will expand the horizons of his profession.

10

Is Patty Hearst in There?

The afternoon of May 17, 1974, three heavily armed SWAT teams moved into position around a one-story stucco house in south Los Angeles. They had traced a van to the area, a van that had been used by the radical group calling itself the Symbionese Liberation Army, kidnappers of the twenty-year-old heiress Patricia Campbell Hearst. An elderly black woman in the neighborhood, Mrs. Mary Carr, had informed a patrolman that a black man, a white man and some white women were in the house at 1466 East Fifty-fourth Street.

The long search for Patty Hearst was over.

The SWAT teams were taking no chances. They were armed with automatic rifles in addition to shotguns and tear-gas weapons. But they knew that the SLA was also heavily armed with automatic rifles, capable of firing a thousand rounds a minute, as well as an arsenal of other rifles, shotguns and pistols.

Still, the police believed, the SLA must know it could not escape. The house was surrounded front and back, and the whole area sealed off. They would have to listen to reason. At 5:44 P.M., a SWAT team leader called to the SLA members over his bullhorn.

"People in the yellow stucco house with the stone porch, this is the Los Angeles Police Department. Come out with your hands up, and you will not be harmed."

A minute passed, then another. Suddenly the front door opened and a small boy stood blinking in the sunlight. A man followed him out. Both lived in the house which had been taken over by the SLA.

When the two were clear, the SWAT team leader repeated his message. No response. A helicopter circled overhead, throngs of neighbors crowded against barricades, reporters and television crews waited tensely for the door to open again—and for Patty Hearst, the most celebrated hostage of the century, to emerge with her captors.

But there was no sign of any activity. The shabby yellow bungalow seemed almost empty. The SWAT team leader made one more bullhorn call, and when there was still no response he gestured to a flak-jacketed team member, who knelt and fired a tear-gas cannister through a front window of the house. A crash of glass, and then choking white smoke billowed outside.

Incredibly, the tear gas had no effect.

"They must have gas masks in there," the SWAT commander said to his deputy. "This is going to be tough." He gave the signal to launch a second tear-gas cannister, hoping that the gas might saturate and overwhelm the filters in the masks.

The tear-gas grenade crashed through a second window—and then what the newspapers called a "war" suddenly erupted. Automatic rifle fire from the house poured out in deadly waves. Police and spectators dove to the ground. Others scrambled for cover. Hundreds of bullets struck cars and houses across the street. The SWAT teams returned fire, riddling the house, and live television transmitted the battle scene throughout the nation.

In San Francisco, William Randolph Hearst, Jr., and his wife watched the scene in horror. Their daughter was in that house—and the police were firing hundreds of bullets into it!

The nightmare which had begun for the Hearst family months before, when their daughter was dragged screaming from a Berkeley apartment by two men and a woman, reached its agonizing climax one minute later when they saw the little house in which Patty Hearst was a hostage of the SLA suddenly explode into flames.

The self-styled Symbionese Liberation Army had first come to public notice in connection with the murder of Dr. Marcus Foster, superintendent of the Oakland schools, who was slain on November 6, 1973. A few days later the SLA took "credit" for the murder and announced the existence of its "army" in a bristling declaration of war: "We of the SLA do now by the rights of our children and by the Force of Arms, and with every drop of blood Declare Revolutionary War against the Fascist Capitalist Class. . . ."

Just over two months later, January 10, 1974, San Francisco police fought a highway gun battle with Russell Little and Joseph Remiro, whose van they had stopped. The van was filled with SLA literature, and the material led police to a house which had been set on fire just before they arrived. When the fire was extinguished, the police discovered stacks of pamphlets on urban guerrilla warfare, boxes of ammunition—and a device used to cap bullets with cyanide. A variety of acids and poisons, gas masks, makeup kits, disguises and maps were also found, as were notebooks with names that would eventually lead to the identification of the members of this strange revolutionary army: Nancy Ling Perry, William Wolfe, Camilla Hall, Angela Atwood, Patricia Soltysik—and Donald DeFreeze, a black convict who had escaped from Soledad Prison.

Scrapbooks also found in the house contained, in alphabetical order, the names, resumés and photographs of prominent Bay Area businessmen who were targets of the SLA, including William Randolph Hearst, Jr. And in one of the notebooks were these lines, to which no one paid any attention at the time: "At U.C.—daughter of Hearst—that bitch's daughter —junior art student. Patricia Campbell Hearst. On the night of the full moon . . . can you make up a team-work game?"

The trappings of a full-scale underground army in that house caused the FBI to begin to investigate the SLA. Still, there was official skepticism. Since the Manson murders in Los Angeles, the hippie movement had faded away. San Francisco and the neighboring University of California at Berkeley, which had been the spirited center of the movement, were now quiet. No riots. No class boycotts. No militants threatening to burn buildings. So the emergence of the SLA puzzled the FBI. Was it just a few crackpots with grandiloquent ideas, who called themselves an "army"? Some even doubted that the so-called SLA had anything to do with the killing of Marcus Foster. After all, Foster, a respected black leader, was hardly a member of the "Fascist Capitalist Class."

So the police did nothing to alert the targets named on the SLA hit list, nor did they warn Patty Hearst.

On February 4, 1974, a "night of the full moon," the SLA struck. At nine-thirty that night, Steven Weed, a young graduate student, and his fiancée, Patty Hearst, were studying in the apartment they shared. There was a knock on the door. A young white woman in a trench coat stood in the doorway, her head downcast. She said she had just had a car accident and wanted to use their telephone. Before Weed could answer, two black men armed with rifles shoved the woman aside. "Down on the floor," one of them commanded Weed, pointing a gun at his head. Weed went down on one knee and was kicked, and kicked again, until he fell prone. The woman tied his wrists behind his back.

Meanwhile Patty Hearst had been shoved into the kitchen, where the intruders demanded she tell them the location of her "safe." She said there wasn't any safe. Then a Japanese-American student in a neighboring apartment, Steve Suenaga, heard the noise and came over. He was dragged into the apartment, thrown to the floor, and tied up next to Weed.

In the commotion Weed jumped to his feet, charged into one of his captors, and then ran through the living room yelling. At any second he expected to be shot. But his shouts caused a different reaction. The intruders let him escape through the back door while they kidnapped the prize, Patty Hearst.

Outside, Weed managed to untie his wrists, but by the time he ran up an alley to the front of the building it was too late. The three abductors were carrying Patty Hearst, kicking and crying for help, out of the house, and were spraying the building with automatic gunfire. As they threw Patty Hearst into the trunk of a convertible, one of the men saw three students run out onto the porch of a house and sent them to the floor with a round of automatic fire. Then, tires squealing, the car raced off into the night.

The SLA had chosen its first hostage wisely if it wanted publicity. For Patty Hearst was a member of a very rich and socially prominent family. Her grandfather, William Randolph Hearst, had been one of the most famous and flamboyant newspaper publishers in this country's history. A movie classic, *Citizen Kane*, had immortalized him on film. His sons, one of whom, William Randolph Hearst, Jr., was Patty's father, were less flamboyant but still active in the management of the family's vast communications empire.

Three days after she was kidnapped, the SLA formally claimed responsibility for the abduction of Patty Hearst and issued its demands in a tape-recorded communiqué from Donald DeFreeze, the escaped convict who now called himself "Cinque," after Joseph

Cinque, the eighteenth-century African who led a mutiny in Cuba, where he had been delivered as a slave. Cinque demanded that William Randolph Hearst, Jr., donate seventy dollars to every poor Californian and concluded his communiqué ominously: "I am not a savage killer and madman . . . and we do hold a high moral value on life. But I am quite willing to carry out the execution of your daughter to save starving men, women and children of every race."

And then, as millions of enthralled Americans listened to the tape on television, the frightened voice of Patty Hearst was heard for the first time since she had been kidnapped: "Mom, Dad, I'm okay. I had a few scrapes and stuff, but they washed them up and they're getting okay. I think you can tell that I'm not really terrified or anything. Try not to worry so much. I know it's hard. I heard that Mom is really upset and that everybody is at home, and I hope this puts you a little at ease. . . ."

DeFreeze had classified as "poor" every Californian with a Social Security, welfare or pension card. It would take more than four hundred million dollars to fulfill the SLA demand. Hearst donated two million in food to the "poor." But this was denounced by the SLA as "a few crumbs to the people." In another communiqué, Cinque said that Hearst not only had "hundreds and hundreds of millions of dollars" but was a personal friend of such people as Howard Hughes and the Shah of Iran. Then he finished in an angry voice: "You do indeed know me. You have always known me. I'm that nigger you have hunted and feared night and day. I'm that nigger you have killed hundreds of people in the vain hope of finding.

. . . I'm the nigger that hunts you now. . . . Death to the fascist insect that preys upon the life of the people."

The fury in his voice was chilling, but once again it was Patty Hearst's voice that fascinated people. "Today is the nineteenth, and yesterday the Shah of Iran had two people executed at dawn," she said. Nothing more than that robotlike statement. But the implication was immediately understood. The Shah of Iran, Hearst's friend, had killed two people yesterday; the SLA could execute one.

The SLA demanded four million dollars more for the poor. Hearst said yes, but only if his daughter was released first. And the next tape-recorded communiqué from the SLA revealed for the first time a different Patty Hearst. She sounded angry at her parents and said, "I don't know who influenced you not to comply with the good-faith gestures. . . . I no longer fear the SLA, only the FBI and certain people in the government who stand to gain anything by my death."

From that moment on, a new mystery emerged. Had a rich young college girl suddenly turned into a revolutionary comrade? It was unbelievable—but the next months would bring one shock after another.

On April 3, just two months after she had been kidnapped, Patty Hearst announced that she had joined the SLA. Her new name was Tania. "I have been given the choice of being released in a safe area or joining the forces of the SLA and fighting for my freedom and the freedom of all oppressed people," she said. "I have chosen to stay and fight."

Apparently, the SLA needed money to pursue that fight. For on April 15 Patty Hearst, along with seven others, held up the Hibernian Bank in San Francisco's Sunset district. Bank cameras showed her holding a semiautomatic rifle. A few weeks later the FBI, acting on a tip, raided an SLA hideout in San Francisco, only to find they were too late. On a wall, among other writings, were these words: "PATRIA A MUERTE, VEN-CEREMOS." (Country [of] death, we shall overcome.) It was signed "Tania."

Then the SLA, and its famous hostage, disappeared, only to surface again in Los Angeles on May 16. A young man and a woman were caught shoplifting in an Inglewood sporting-goods store. An employee followed them out and even managed to put handcuffs on one. But suddenly bullets spattered all around him. Patty Hearst, the new revolutionary, was firing from a van to cover the escape of her SLA comrades.

The trail of that shooting from one stolen van to another led a day later to the stucco house on East Fifty-fourth Street in Los Angeles, a house that in a matter of moments had been reduced to burning rubble.

SWAT gunners still crouched behind cars when my staff and I arrived at the scene of the shootout. I saw the fiery ashes of a building that had burned to the ground, and heard the *crack! crack! crack!* of ammunition still detonating in the ruins. No one could be alive in those ashes, I thought.

Reporters behind the barricades at the scene were in an uproar concerning one question: Was Patty Hearst in that house? If so, she was certainly dead.

It would be my job to find out just who was in that house, which would be difficult enough, but I immediately recognized the existence of another problem. The house was next to a black community. The leader of the SLA was black. And I knew from reports that the LAPD had poured hundreds of rounds of ammunition into the house, eventually causing an explosion of fire which killed everyone inside. No one could deny that the SLA had fired at the police, but to black citizens the reactions of the SWAT teams might seem excessive and even have a racist aspect.

Thus I knew I had two important missions on that particular day: not only to identify the bodies, including Patty Hearst's, but to find out just how the SLA fugitives had died.

Someone handed me a yellow slicker, and I started toward the burning ashes of the house with my staff and an LAPD officer. Bob Dambacher, my assistant chief investigator, immediately discovered a charred body about ten feet from the southeast corner of the house. The police officer said that a young woman had burst from the house in a ball of flames.

A painstaking step-by-step photographic documentation of this first body began. And when my staff had finished the job, I crouched beside it and noticed something odd: the melted remains of a gas mask on her face. No identification was possible at that time.

But the mask showed that the other SLA members might have worn similar equipment. If so, they had prepared for a battle to the death, and that would be a point in justification of the SWAT teams' actions. I also noticed that a pistol lay beside the body. And the woman wore boots and layers of clothing, not all of which was burned. Had she perished from fire and smoke inhalation, or had she been shot when she ran from the house? I couldn't detect bullet holes in the blackened body, but an autopsy would reveal the cause of death.

We walked into the debris of the house, where firemen were carefully removing burned wood, melted iron, and ashes. The sounds of exploding ammunition occasionally came from the smoking wreckage, startling everyone. I knew that the safest plan would be to call off our search until the last smoldering ember had been extinguished. But Patty Hearst's body might be in those ashes; in fact, there was no doubt that she was one of the victims as far as the LAPD, I myself and all of America were concerned. So, leaving aside the pressure of the media, I decided to continue out of consideration for the Hearst family.

In the southwest corner of the building another body had been uncovered by the firemen. This too was a female, fully clothed and booted, with a melted gas mask covering her face and an M-1 automatic rifle still clutched in one blackened hand. Was this Patty Hearst? I didn't know. Her face was so badly burned that she was unrecognizable.

Very carefully, conscious of the live ammunition, firemen continued to remove the scorched debris. The LAPD officer told me the house had been only one story, consisting of two bedrooms, a living room, a kitchen and a bathroom. No basement—but he said there was a crawl space under the house about eighteen inches high, and some of the gunfire had seemed to come from vent holes in the foundation wall around that crawl space.

From the corner of the house where the bathroom had been, my top forensic photographer-investigator,

Bill Lystrup, who later became chief of the Forensic Support Bureau, suddenly gave us a signal. More bodies, covered with pipes and debris, had been discovered in the crawl space beneath the bathroom. The investigator removed the wreckage, and I observed a bizarre scene. One decedent seemed to be kneeling over a second, totally burned. A third decedent lay sprawled next to the other two with a .38 snubnosed revolver beside them. The kneeling body was that of a woman wearing a cartridge belt which still held live ammunition. She too could have been Patty Hearst.

It had become dark, and the Fire Department illuminated the scene with floodlights. We were bathed in an eerie twilight as the search went on, while outside the lighted arena the press and a crowd of hundreds still waited.

I instructed my staff representative, Bob Dambacher, to contact the FBI. "Tell them I want the dental charts on all of the SLA fugitives at my office at midnight. We'll set up a special office for the FBI in the forensic center."

"What about fingerprints?" he asked.

"From what I've seen, the fingers are all burned. But they can check the bodies when we get to the autopsy room, just in case."

The firemen searched the ruins for three more hours, with no result. We had recovered five bodies, and I dispatched them in a medical examiner's van to the Forensic Science Center, where we would begin work immediately. We could not wait. Three of the bodies were women, and either of two of them might be Patty Hearst.

* * *

Dr. Gerald Vale was an athletic, white-haired, handsome man, unique in his background. He was not only a graduate of dental school, but also had earned a law degree. I had appointed him as chief of the forensic-dentistry division, and he had trained many forensic odontologists.

We met in my office at midnight. Vale had obtained from the FBI, which was working in a special office in the building, the dental charts of all suspected members of the SLA—and of Patty Hearst, who, fortunately, had had dental X rays taken just two weeks before she was kidnapped. I instructed Vale to have the jaw surgically removed from each victim before he X-rayed it. That was necessary because we had to duplicate exactly the angle of the X-ray photography taken by the victims' dentists with our own X rays in order to be absolutely certain of a match. By surgically removing the jaw, along with any partial bridges, crowns and fillings, we could X-ray with more precision.

Dental matching has always been a very useful tool to forensic scientists. Each set of teeth has a unique alignment. Some teeth are crooked, some are missing —including wisdom teeth, which erupt (break through the skin surface) when a person is twenty to twenty-five years old, thus aiding in the determination of the decedent's age if that is relevant. Other individual characteristics include the spaces between teeth and the degree of absorption of the teeth into the bone structure of the jaw. Cavities also are unique. And fillings are not exactly alike in configuration or in their location.

Dr. Vale and his staff, I knew, would very carefully compare their X rays of the dental features of all of the SLA decedents with the dental charts obtained from the FBI, looking for a match, and I awaited the results in my office. I remember the next few hours as a blur. Telephone call after telephone call from the LAPD, the FBI, the press—all eager to know if Patty Hearst was among the victims. Finally, at 6 A.M., I went down to the lab where Vale and his staff were working.

"First, the bad news," he said. "So far we've positively identified only two victims from their dental charts." He paused, then said, "But the good news is that Patty Hearst's dental chart doesn't match any of the X rays we took. She wasn't in that house."

I could hardly believe it. Patty Hearst had been with the SLA for months. Just the day before, she had been among them at the Inglewood sporting-goods store. Now five SLA members had died in a shootout—and their hostage was absent?

"And by the way," Vale said. "I almost forgot the really bad news."

I tensed. "What?"

"Donald DeFreeze wasn't in that house either."

Again I was startled. The SLA leader was missing, too? "Don't his dental charts match any of your X rays?" I asked.

"No. We obtained his chart from the prison dental office, and they don't compare at all. But from our past experience, prison records are notoriously unreliable."

It was an unusual situation. As far as we knew, there had been only one black male in the SLA: De-

Freeze. And of the three as yet unidentified bodies, one was a black male. It almost had to be Cinque, which meant that the prison records were wrong. But if the prison records were correct, DeFreeze, the most feared of the SLA militants, was still on the loose.

I spoke immediately to the FBI agents at work in the building and asked them to pass on the good news about Patty Hearst to her parents. Then I told them we hadn't been able to identify DeFreeze. "Have you had any luck with the fingerprints?" I asked.

I knew that the fire had almost completely destroyed the victim's fingertips, so I was surprised when the FBI agent replied, "Sure, we've got De-Freeze for you."

"From fingerprints?"

"Not exactly. We'll come over to your office and show you."

A few moments later in my office, I was looking at huge magnified photographs which seemed to show white bands with wavy lines. "Precisely what are they?" I asked.

"Strips of unburned skin from DeFreeze's fingers," the FBI agent said. "They match his prints."

It was true. What the FBI fingerprint technicians had skillfully accomplished was an example of pure forensic science at its best.

With intense heat, hand muscles contract, and the fingers curl up into charred claws. But in the process tiny strips of skin in the inner folds of the finger joints may be preserved from the fire—as was the case with DeFreeze.

When fingerprints of DeFreeze had been taken in prison, his fingers were laid flat on ink pads. Thus the

FBI had photographs of his fingers in their entirety, including the strips of skin at the inner folds. Under intense magnification, the FBI was then able to compare the strips of skin in the finger creases of the decedent with a copy of a fingerprint card of DeFreeze, and to find a precise match of the creases.

By nine that morning we had identified all of the victims, and at a press conference I told reporters that Patty Hearst had not been inside that house of death on East Fifty-fourth Street. Newspapers and television carried the news of her miraculous escape all that day. But then the next morning we had another shock.

A sixth body had been uncovered in the debris. A woman.

I was horrified. Just yesterday I had relayed word to Mr. and Mrs. Hearst that their daughter was alive. And now another unidentified female had been found dead in that house. It had to be Patty Hearst.

Once again reporters clamored for more information. And I realized the extent of the despair of the Hearsts when I received a telephone call from Ronald Reagan, then Governor of California. He said he was calling on behalf of the Hearsts. In his words, "It's devastating to the family. Can you help them?"

I said I would personally call Mr. and Mrs. Hearst as soon as we learned the identity of the last victim.

I immediately returned with my staff to the scene of the shootout, where we found that someone had placed a lonely bouquet of flowers in front of the burned-out house. We learned that the sixth victim had been deeply buried in debris in the southwest corner of the house. The LAPD's Special Investigation Division had been examining the debris by the grid system, and this corner had been the last to be thoroughly searched. I ordered the body transported back to the center.

There, in an autopsy room, Dr. Vale began his work, carefully positioning the X-ray camera for photos of the jaw of the sixth victim. We had to wait until the X rays were developed, then we crowded around anxiously as they were compared with those of Patty Hearst.

No match. The X rays duplicated those of Camilla Hall, another member of the SLA. Patty Hearst, once again, had proved to be miraculously alive.

I was a bit frayed when I picked up the telephone and called the number in San Francisco that Ronald Reagan had given me. A man answered the phone. "Mr. Hearst?" I said.

"Yes."

"This is Dr. Noguchi, coroner of Los Angeles County. I would like to tell you that the sixth victim is not your daughter."

There was a pause, and then, "Oh, thank God."

The next voice was a woman's. Mrs. Hearst wanted to hear the news herself. I told her, and she started to weep with joy.

The victims who had died in the shootout, in addition to Camilla Hall and Donald DeFreeze, were Nancy Ling Perry, Angela Atwood, William Wolfe and Patricia Soltysik. Autopsies on their bodies revealed that two of the six had died not from SWAT team bullets, but from flames and smoke inhalation. Members of the black community (and many other concerned citizens as well) were already charging that the SWAT teams had overreacted in what some were calling the "SLA massacre." Therefore I believed it was necessary for the public to know what had actually happened in that battle. And I decided to go back to the scene and try to re-create, from forensic evidence, the last-minute actions of the SLA militants. My plan to do so aroused good-humored skepticism from some members of the media. The house was now only a pile of ashes, with a few foundation stones poking through. How could I show every militant's movements in a building that wasn't even there anymore?

From eyewitness reports and certain tests and examinations that had already been made at the scene, I had an overall impression of the events of that afternoon. And now, as I stood once more near the rubble of the house on East Fifty-fourth Street, I could see in my mind's eye a SWAT team member kneeling to fire a tear-gas cannister into the house, then another—and I could picture what happened next.

As soon as the second tear-gas cannister was fired, the SLA had begun shooting, riddling with bullets the cars parked in front of the house. Because they were stationary and had many surfaces, the cars showed perfectly the trajectory of the bullets, thus revealing the location of the guns that had fired them. From those tracks, and from recovered bullets, I knew that two of the SLA militants (and no more than two) had fired from slightly different angles out of the front windows of the house as the battle began. Almost immediately, however, the other four militants found themselves faced with a crisis—fire.

I walked through the debris to the area where the front bedroom had been. In the ashes I saw a black-

'ened gasoline can. I picked it up and observed a bullet hole in its side. Now I knew how the fire that destroyed the house had begun. A bullet from the SWAT team had punctured the gasoline can, and the leaking gas had been ignited by the tremendous heat given off when a tear-gas cannister exploded.

From an examination of the bodies at the scene the day of the shootout, I knew that the SLA militants had dressed themselves for combat. They wore many layers of clothes, boots, and even gas masks to deal with the expected tear gas. But they were not prepared for fire. One, and only one, militant panicked. Nancy Ling Perry's clothes caught fire as the flames spread, and she tried to escape from the rear of the house. We had found her charred body outside.

But the autopsy had revealed that there were bullet holes in her body. Why had the SWAT team fired at a person in flames? The autopsy of Camilla Hall told us the reason. Hall had died with a bullet hole in her forehead. Almost certainly, she had been firing at the SWAT team, covering for Nancy Ling Perry, and the answering fusillade struck both of them.

Near the body of Hall was the first victim who had died from smoke inhalation and fire, Angela Atwood. The fact that she had not been found with the other three SLA members who were then still alive showed me that she too was involved in the Perry breakout. From the position of her body when discovered, it appeared to me that she must have tried to pull Camilla Hall back to safety after she was hit. By then Atwood was surrounded by flames, her clothes on fire. She could have dashed out at that point, but she did not, and burned to death.

With a fire raging throughout the house, consuming all with flames, the SWAT teams outside had ceased firing. No one could live in that inferno. But inside, three SLA members were making a desperate—and ingenious—effort to survive. And I knew they had lived for an incredibly long time, because they kept firing at police from the crawl space beneath the house.

But there was no entrance to that crawl space. How had they ended up there and avoided the fire for so long? I roamed through the wreckage until I reached the debris of the bathroom, where I saw evidence that a large hole had been chopped in the floor. An ax had been found near the hole. Then I noticed something else odd in the ruins. I crouched to examine the blackened bathtub and observed that both faucets were stuck in the on position. I found the faucets in the sink also on. And at that moment I was able to picture the final apocalypse.

When the fire exploded in a front bedroom and spread, three of the SLA—DeFreeze, Wolfe and Soltysik—had run to the bathroom. There they drenched their clothes in water, then chopped a hole in the floor. And before climbing into the crawl space they turned all the water faucets in the bathtub and sink to the full on position. They reasoned that the water would overflow and pour down into the crawl space, flooding it and protecting them from the raging fire above.

In their drenched clothes, with water gushing down on them, they were able to continue shooting from a house engulfed in flames. But the fire was unrelenting. Plumbing pipes melted and twisted, shutting off the water. The flames licked closer, and they knew they must die—if they chose to stay.

Stay they did, even as the gas masks melted on their faces. William Wolfe died from smoke inhalation and burns. Patricia Soltysik died from a combination of smoke inhalation, burns and multiple gunshot wounds. Donald DeFreeze died of a gunshot wound.

Thus the SLA had perished. And by using basic forensic science I was able to establish the order in which all of them died. Fire creates smoke, and smoke and carbon monoxide are inhaled. Therefore, the victim with the most carbon monoxide in his blood, DeFreeze, died last; the one with the least, Hall, perished first. And with reasonable certainty I could state the exact order of death of the others by the same principle.

Symbolically, Cinque—Donald DeFreeze—was the final SLA member to die. And when I found what might have been gunpowder burns on his forehead, I first thought that he, like Hitler, had killed himself when the end was near. But tests in our laboratory revealed that there were metallic elements in the fatal wound which were not present in the .38 bullets in DeFreeze's own pistol. I believed, therefore, that the gunpowder burns came from exploding ammunition near DeFreeze.

The fiery *Götterdämmerung* of the SLA gave all Americans a frightening insight into the potential of political terrorism. Educated young people, inspired by a political belief, however naïve or chaotic, would not shrink from any peril, including death by fire, in pursuit of their goals.

As I said when I released my report to the public on the last moments of the SLA: "They died compulsively. They chose to stay under the floor as the fire burned out. In all my years as a coroner I've never before seen this kind of conduct in the face of flames."

The strength of their dedication was so incredible to me that I ordered a psychological autopsy to be performed. And we learned that political terrorists believe that the most effective way to arouse public sympathy for their cause is death. Therefore they are not afraid of dying, and that's why conventional police tactics fail when used against them. Faced with a choice to surrender to the authorities or to die in action, they will almost always choose to die.

My reconstruction of the last moments of the SLA helped cool public resentment against the SWAT teams. The public now knew that the militants would never have surrendered. Even engulfed in flames, they kept firing, trying to kill the "oppressors," to the end. That legacy of terrorism is still with us today as it rose from the inferno of a little house in south Los Angeles.

11

Forensic Science at Work

Our work in the SLA shootout brought the Los Angeles County Medical Examiner's Office nationwide publicity, and suddenly I was besieged by magazine and newspaper reporters intent on writing about me in particular. In the same week, both *Time* and *Newsweek* featured articles on the American coroner of Japanese descent in Los Angeles. Interestingly, most of those journalists seemed to be fascinated by a phase of my work which was apparently little known to them: forensic pathology with a related investigative approach. And they portrayed me as a Japanese version of Sherlock Holmes, an Oriental sleuth who specialized in solving "impossible" murders through hunches and seemingly invisible clues.

Flattering, but exaggerated. I'm no Sherlock Holmes—nor even a Charlie Chan. But after those articles appeared I began to receive requests from all over the country to solve mysterious homicides. If the challenge to forensic science was so intriguing that I thought it valuable to proceed, I would do so. But I couldn't, of course, accommodate most of the requests, because I was working long hours on a full-time basis as a chief medical examiner. And there were more than enough mysterious homicides right there in Los Angeles.

JUST A HUNCH

The pretty young blonde lay stretched on the floor beside her bed, a small bullet hole in the center of her forehead oozing blood. Detectives investigating the crime asked neighbors in the apartment house if they had heard shots. The answer was no.

It seemed like a typical Hollywood tragedy. The blonde was an actress just starting out on her career. LAPD detectives knew from experience how vulnerable these young women were to sharpsters, con men and criminals. Desperate to make a breakthrough in the motion picture industry, they often fell prey to Hollywood sharks—and violence.

But the case was to prove far from typical. My deputy, who performed the autopsy, called me to the table upon which the young actress lay. "It's strange," he said. "The police say she was shot, but there's no bullet in her brain—and no exit wound through which it escaped."

I was stumped. I checked with the investigator who had spoken to the homicide detectives. He said that no weapons had been recovered at the scene and no one had heard any shots. But there *was* the bullet hole in her forehead, identical to thousands I had seen, down to the typical ring of abrasion with the skin scraped in around the edges of the wound.

I told the deputy to store the decedent's body until we did further investigating, because—as was plain—the manner and cause of death were unknown. And when I told homicide detectives of the mystery, they were surprised and frustrated. "How can we find the creep who did this if we don't even know how she was killed?"

The case haunted me until it became almost an obsession. Still, no explanation came to me, and, as the days passed, the case of the young actress receded into the backlog of other homicide investigations, destined, it seemed, to be stamped forever "Cause of Death Undetermined."

Then one brisk December day in downtown Los Angeles, I was shopping for Christmas gifts during my lunch hour and stopped in front of a boutique. A few other shoppers looked into the window beside me, for there were beautiful stylish clothes on display. I remember it was a green blouse that had caught my attention. It would look good on my wife.

The blouse was on a mannequin, and I couldn't see a price tag. But as I looked for it on the floor at the mannequin's feet all thoughts of the blouse vanished forever. In an instant I changed from a civilian shopper into a medical examiner. And what I was looking at now was not a gift but a possible murder weapon.

Or was I being ridiculous? The "weapon" I saw was a woman's spike-heeled shoe. Could such a shoe have made the wound in the young actress's forehead that we thought was a bullet hole?

Inside the store I inspected a similar shoe while a woman sales clerk stared at me quizzically. For instead of admiring the shoe itself I examined only the tip of its heel. It may be fantastic, I thought, but that heel will fit.

It was just a hunch. In fact, before calling an LAPD detective, I delayed for some hours after returning to my office. "It may seem foolish to you," I said tentatively, "but I saw something that might possibly have caused the wound."

"What?"

"A woman's spike-heeled shoe."

Silence. Then the detective said, "Dr. Noguchi, you're kidding us."

"It's just an idea, and maybe I'm pressing," I said. "But why don't you search the neighborhood for a spike-heeled shoe? You have nothing to lose."

I believe the detective thought I had lost my mind, although he didn't say it. But the tone of amusement in his voice when he reluctantly agreed to make the "fantasy" search told it all.

A few hours later, the detective called me back. In an empty lot a block away from the scene, detectives had found a woman's spike-heeled shoe with dried blood on its heel. When we tested the blood, we discovered that it matched the victim's type. And the metal tip of the heel, under microscopic examination, exactly matched the entrance wound in her forehead.

We had found the weapon. And we were even able to discover a clue to the possible identity of the murderer, if the killer was the person who had worn the shoe. Chemical substances known as antigens, to which the blood develops antibodies, enable forensic scientists to determine whether the blood type is A, B, AB or O. Other body fluids, such as saliva, urine and perspiration, can also be analyzed for blood typing by the presence of antigens. In this case, sweat absorbed into the leather of the spike-heeled shoe told us the blood type—but not the identity—of the probable murderer.

Who would kill a person by striking her with a woman's shoe? The police pondered the question. Assuming that a man would be unlikely to use such a shoe—and a woman normally wouldn't have the strength to kill someone with it—the LAPD came up with a possible answer to the mystery. A transvestite or a man who had undergone a sex-change operation could have murdered the victim. Such a person would have had the strength—and many such people had fetishes, so the police postulated, about high-heeled shoes.

Those were assumptions I was unwilling to make without further evidence of the killer's identity. But if the LAPD was right, this "typical" Hollywood tragedy took on an entirely different complexion, especially after the police came up with a hot suspect who *was* a transvestite. Nor did the case have a typical Hollywood ending, in which justice is done. Police searched for the transvestite for weeks, but were never able to find him. We had discovered "the manner and cause of death" of the young actress, but not who had killed her.

THE CASE OF THE BARKING DOG
One day I received an unusual telephone call about a possible murder. It did not come from my friends at the homicide division or from the DA's Office. In-

stead, it came from the Humane Society, which takes care of pets. It seems they had freed a dog locked in an abandoned house, and they suspected foul play unrelated to pets. I went to the house, which was in Hollywood, and found the LAPD also on hand. When I entered the house I saw why. There were bloodstains on the walls and floor of the bathroom.

The LAPD had been told by neighbors that two men lived in the house together, but neither had been seen for days. And there were no personal effects or clothing in the house, which had apparently been abandoned. The barking of the dog left inside had caused neighbors to call the Humane Society.

While the LAPD searched for other clues to the identity of the two men, I looked around the bathroom. There was an unusual pungent smell in that room. I examined the tub and saw that its interior was yellow-stained. And at that moment I felt a little chill of horror as I realized the possible significance of the smell coupled with that stain. I ordered the whole bathroom dug up.

A few hours later the tub had been removed and part of the bathroom floor was gone, replaced by a trench six feet deep. I stood on the edge of it, keeping clear of the flying dirt from the shovels of the workmen beneath.

As I watched, the workmen uncovered the drainpipe and opened the trap. "Just a moment," I said. They stopped and looked up. "Can you give me a hand?" I asked. They assisted me down into the trench, where I went to the drain trap and crouched beside it.

There I observed a tiny object, covered with silt,

caught in the trap. I recovered it for closer examination, cleaned it off—and saw it was a human tooth.

Examining the rest of the drain trap closely, I found a second tooth. And with the two teeth in the palm of my hand, I knew that the ghoulish suspicion I had had when I first saw the yellowish stain in the tub was correct. A human body had been dissolved in acid in the tub and then washed down the drain.

By late afternoon, the LAPD had discovered the identities of the two men who had lived in the house. Both were missing. I told them to trace the men's dentists to try to match the two teeth I had found in the drain trap. "But for a faster route," I said, "see if you can find which of the two men had access to sulfuric acid."

The LAPD did that, and discovered that one of the men worked as an accountant in an industrial plant which utilized sulfuric acid in its manufacturing process. A few days later, acting on a tip, they found and confronted the man. He told the police a chilling story. He and his roommate had had an argument over rent money, a fight erupted, and the roommate was accidentally killed when he fell and cracked his head against the tub.

Fearing he would be accused of murder, the man decided to dispose of the body, and he knew just how to do it. First he chopped the body into small pieces. Then he went to the plant where he worked and appropriated gallons of sulfuric acid. He brought them to the house and, crouching by the tub, patiently dissolved each and every piece of his roommate's body in the tub, then washed the remains down the drain.

That done, he felt he was safe forever. No one could

accuse him of murder if there was no body. But he had made stupid mistakes. After all the long and painstaking effort to get rid of the body, he left the house in such a hurry that he didn't even wash the bloodstains off the bathroom walls and floor. He also left inside the house a noisy little dog whose barking would eventually bring the police.

And, most significant of all, he was unaware that two teeth in a drain trap six feet below the house would prove to be the corpus delicti.

THE WRONG KNIFE

I was performing an autopsy on a young Mexican in his twenties who had been stabbed to death. An LAPD homicide detective entered the room, carrying a brown paper bag which held the fatal weapon. "Do you want to take a look at it?" he asked.

"No," I said. "I'll tell *you* exactly what it looks like."

I wasn't showing off. It was an opportunity to demonstrate an important forensic technique to the pathology residents who were observing the autopsy. The traditional method of measuring a knife was to pour barium sulfate into the wound and X-ray it. I thought I had found a better way.

I lit a little Bunsen burner and melted some Wood's metal over it, while the detective and the residents watched. Then I selected a wound in the victim's chest above the location of the liver and poured the liquid metal into it. The metal slid down through the wound into the punctured liver. And when it cooled, I removed an exact mold of the tip of the murder weapon. I added the length of this tip to the distance between the liver and the skin surface of the chest. Then I said to the homicide detective, "It's a knife five and a half inches long, one inch wide and one sixteenth of an inch thick."

He smiled and reached into his bag. "Sorry, Dr. Noguchi." He pulled out a much smaller pocketknife, only about three inches in length.

"That's the wrong knife," I said at once.

"Oh, now, come on," the detective said. "We found the knife that killed him right at the scene."

"You don't have the murder weapon," I insisted.

He didn't believe me. But two days later police found a bloodstained knife in a trashcan two blocks from the scene of the crime. That weapon was exactly five and a half inches long, one inch wide and one sixteenth of an inch thick. And the blood on its blade matched the victim's.

It turned out to be the murder weapon. The pocketknife the police discovered at the scene had been used by the victim in self-defense. And two knives indicated a knife fight. Was it part of a gang war? The police investigated and found out that the victim was a member of a mini-gang which was at war with another gang. And through the interrogation of the members of the rival gang, they eventually identified a Mexican teenager as the murderer.

A BONE OF CONTENTION

Torrential rains struck California, rivers and streams overflowed and flooded the canyons. An old rusting Volkswagen which had been invisible in the underbrush in one of those canyons was lifted and deposited in plain sight near a road.

When the LAPD investigated the car, the door on the driver's side was hanging open and nobody was found inside. But the license plate quickly identified the owner of the car: a man who had been missing for years and presumed dead.

The LAPD did not know what to believe. Was it a legitimate fatal accident, with the remains of the owner's body lost in the flood? Or was it perhaps a hoax to establish a *fictitious* death for insurance or other purposes, with the owner assuming a new identity?

Excavation was begun in the canyon, but all that was found was one small piece of bone. The LAPD brought it to our office, where we immediately identified it as a part of a human collarbone, so someone *had* died in the vicinity.

But how to prove, from a small piece of collarbone, that it was indeed the owner of the Volkswagen who had died?

I had a thought: chest X rays. Such X rays, taken to examine the heart or the lungs of a patient, always include the collarbone in the frame of the shot. We asked the owner's wife if her husband had ever been given a chest X ray. She said yes, and soon the X ray was on our desk.

I called in a consultant, forensic radiologist Isaac Sanders, M.D., to examine the bone fragment and the X ray. Was it possible to take new X rays of the bone fragment that could be compared to the owner's X ray and thus prove that he was indeed dead? We discussed the fact that the tension of the muscle and the tissue in the human shoulder must somehow be duplicated if we were to obtain an image of the fragment precise enough for such a comparison.

Dr. Sanders was puzzled about how to do this, until he came up with the idea of placing a water bag on top of the bone fragment to try to simulate soft tissue on the body. When he did that, the X ray of the bone fragment exactly matched the X ray of a segment of the owner's collarbone. From a tiny piece of bone, Dr. Sanders had identified the man.

That forensic feat confirmed the death of the owner of the Volkswagen. And it also resolved any problem the widow may have had with insurance companies which might have suspected a hoax when her husband's body was not found in the car.

THE INVISIBLE MURDER

One of the most ingenious murderers who ever lived was a man who not only planned his homicides elaborately but killed his victims in such a way that there was absolutely no trace of foul play—no weapons, no poison, no marks on the body and, most remarkably, no evidence in the organs and the blood.

Act One of this crime began with a car accident in Long Beach stage-managed by the killer. His nephew, who was riding with him in the car, was thrown against the windshield, suffering chest injuries and cuts in the head. The murderer was uninjured. And the "accident" occurred within a few blocks of a hospital, for that too was part of the murderer's scheme.

Act Two took place in a hospital room, with the unsuspecting nephew bandaged and lying in bed, and his dutiful uncle sitting nearby, consoling him. The nurse who moved in and out of the room saw nothing out of the ordinary. She merely noted that the uncle looked distraught at the pain his nephew was suffering.

The climax of the drama occurred in Act Three, hours after the uncle had left the hospital. A nurse, checking on the nephew, found that he had fallen into a coma. It was incredible. His injuries weren't serious. His X rays had shown there was nothing remarkable. Rushing him to the operating room, doctors made a "burr hole" in his skull. There was no blood in the subdural space between the skull and the brain, which meant there had been no brain injury. Frantic efforts to save his life finally failed. And the bereaved uncle, summoned back to the hospital, broke down and cried.

The following day, a homicide sergeant called my office. "We've got a funny one here, Dr. Noguchi."

"What is it?"

"Well, we don't even know if it's a murder. But we've been told the uncle is going to collect insurance on the death of his nephew."

The sergeant explained the circumstances of the case, then told me the hospital physicians believed strongly that, since brain surgery had revealed no brain trauma, the nephew could not have slipped into a coma without outside help. They suspected that the uncle had injected him with some drug, but they could find no fresh needle marks on his body.

I conducted the forensic investigation, including an autopsy, on the nephew, looking carefully for fresh punctures. His body was unmarked, just as the sergeant had said. And the report from the toxicology laboratory showed absolutely no trace of poison or drugs. So if it was murder, I thought, how had the uncle accomplished it? It was a complete mystery to me.

Meanwhile, the LAPD had asked assistance from the FBI—and discovered from the FBI's files that another insured relative of the uncle, in another state, had died in identical circumstances: first a car crash, then the hospital visit, and finally the coma. Police were now certain the man was a murderer. But how could they prove it when there was absolutely no trace of evidence?

To find out, in what would perhaps be a futile effort, I decided to try to re-create the exact scene in the nephew's hospital room at the time of his uncle's visit. Since the police suspected foul play, nothing had been touched or removed from that room, including the medical equipment that had been used to treat the nephew. When the doctor and the nurses who were on duty at the time were assembled in the room, I said to one of my staff members, "You're the nephew. Lie down on the bed, please." Then I said to the doctor, "You're the uncle. Where did he sit?"

When the doctor moved a chair to the right side of the bed and sat down, I immediately observed that the uncle's access to his nephew's body would have been blocked by the medical equipment that had been used to feed him intravenously. It would have been difficult, if not impossible, to inject him from that location. I was nonplussed. My re-creation of the scene only made the uncle look more innocent.

But then I stepped back to the doorway of the room to survey the scene from a larger angle—and mental lightning struck. Of course, that was it! "He didn't inject the nephew," I said. "He injected the tubing of the intravenous-fluid bottle."

We took the tubing back to our laboratories and examined it under a microscope. There was a fresh puncture in its side.

A needle had made that hole. So now we knew how the uncle had injected the nephew. But since no poison or drug had been in the nephew's body, we still did not know what had killed him. It wasn't until police found that the uncle had once worked in a psychiatric hospital in Los Angeles, giving doses of insulin to patients, that we knew what to look for.

Human insulin is a chemical found naturally in the body and is the substance that regulates blood sugar. The type of "artificial" insulin injected into humans, chiefly in the treatment of diabetes, is obtained from a hog's pancreas. But once it is inside the body, it is impossible to differentiate it from human insulin.

However, there are ways to detect its presence. A low sugar content in the spinal fluid is a presumptive sign of an excessive amount of insulin in the body. So I first made a spinal tap on the nephew's body, analyzed the spinal fluid and found a 10-milligram sugar count compared to the 80- to 100-milligram count which is normal.

Then a radio immune assay test which had been developed by a professor at a local university was performed. In this process hog insulin is injected into a rabbit, which then develops antibodies in its blood. A serum containing these antibodies is "tagged" with radioactive isotopes, and when it is introduced into human blood the antibodies combine with the insulin, thus enabling us to detect its presence. Results of the test performed on the nephew revealed, as I recall, the presence of over eight hundred units of insulin in his blood and body tissue—again well above normal.

That was enough evidence to try and convict the uncle for murder. At his trial, however, only evidence of the murder of his nephew was admitted. But during the penalty phase the District Attorney was able to introduce evidence of no fewer than six other murders the uncle had committed around the country. He made a mistake when he committed his seventh in Los Angeles.

WHO SHOT THE DRIVER?

One night a car careened off a road in the San Gabriel Mountains, out of control, bounced down a hillside, glanced off one tree and then crashed to a halt against another. In the moonlight, the driver's head could be seen through the open car window, tilted forward over the wheel. A bullet hole in his left temple oozed a trickle of blood.

I arrived at the scene just as the body was being placed on a stretcher ready for transfer to the forensic center. "It must have been a sniper," a sheriff's deputy told me. "We're getting more and more of those loonies around here, taking potshots at passing cars."

But his partner had a different idea. "Snipers usually operate on busy highways, not way up in the mountains. I think it was premeditated murder. Somebody shot the driver inside the car while it was parked along the road, then got out and pushed the car over the edge."

I examined the body on the stretcher. "It wasn't a

sniper," I said. "And I doubt that it was murder. It was suicide."

The deputies looked astonished. "There are powder burns on the driver's left temple," I explained, "which means it was a close-contact wound. That would rule out a sniper shooting from long range."

"Okay, but it still could have been murder."

"I doubt it," I said. "If the murderer was inside the car, he would have to have been a contortionist to shoot the driver through the left temple. Of course, I can't rule out the possibility that someone shot him from close range through the open window from outside the car. But I believe the driver shot himself. Then, when the car was rolling down the hillside, either he dropped the gun out the window in a recoil action or it was jolted out of his hand."

Now the deputies were even more skeptical. It seemed unlikely that anyone would be so intent on suicide that he would shoot himself as he was driving his car.

"There's one way to find out," I suggested. "Search the hillside along the car's tire tracks. I think you'll find the gun."

Reluctantly, the deputies made the search. They found a pistol lying in the underbrush by the tire tracks, just below the road. The fingerprints on its grip were those of the driver. He *had* committed suicide.

TIME OF DEATH

A small boy disappeared from his home, and five weeks later his body was found stuffed into a meter box adjacent to a Hollywood freeway. The decomposition of the body indicated that the boy had been dead for a long time. But how long?

The time of death became critically important because the man who was suspected of committing the crime was at home three hours after the time of the boy's disappearance and was seen continually until the body was found. He even helped search for the boy. But the District Attorney's Office could not prosecute the man because of insufficient evidence and asked me for my assistance.

In viewing the body, I saw a great number of maggots in different stages of development. Entomology shows us that the blowfly, the species to which these maggots belong, undergoes a complete metamorphosis in its development. Like a butterfly, it changes from the maggot stage, analogous to the caterpillar, into a cocoon, from which it eventually emerges as a fly. I knew, too, that this metamorphosis takes place within a specific length of time, so that I could establish the time of the boy's death by estimating the time it would take maggots to reach the stage of development in which they had been found on the boy's body.

For the next several weeks, my associates must have thought I was taking up a new hobby as I experimented with countless generations of blowflies in the laboratory. One, in fact, commented that I had gone "buggy." But finally I was able to determine, under conditions that duplicated the condition of the boy's body, the age of the maggots that had been found on it. And from that I was able to establish the time of the boy's death. It was within three hours of the time of his disappearance. On that evidence, it was therefore possible that the suspect could have committed the crime. The District Attorney's Office brought the man to trial and secured his conviction.

BLOOD AND SEX

On December 19, 1972, Detective John Rogan of the New York City Police Department and his partner, George Merrihue, viewed a body in an apartment in the Bronx. The victim, Minnie Goldfaden, was lying on the living-room floor with bruise marks on her throat that indicated strangulation.

Edward Goldfaden, her thirty-seven-year-old son, took the detectives to the kitchen and pointed out an area where the linoleum floor covering had been ripped open. "She hid her cash under there," he said. "Now the money's gone."

"Who knew about it?"

"Only me and my brother Leonard."

The detectives noticed there were triple locks on the apartment door, and there was no sign of the door having been forced. The victim had obviously let the murderer into the apartment. And that murderer had to be either Edward or Leonard Goldfaden, the detectives thought.

They were just about to depart to interrogate Leonard when Rogan saw something on the floor beside the victim's right foot. He knelt down and picked up a black leather button, which he put into an evidence envelope and took with him.

Leonard Goldfaden was a man in his early thirties. While the detectives talked to him in his apartment, Rogan noticed a black leather coat draped over a couch. A button on its right sleeve was missing.

The detectives took the coat, and Leonard, to the

police station. There the police forensic laboratory put the coat under a microscope—and discovered tiny traces of dried blood on its lapel. The button also had blood on it.

Leonard Goldfaden told the detectives that the blood on his coat had come from a fight in a bar and then would answer no more questions.

He was booked for the murder of his mother, but a few days later the police received a shock. The New York Medical Examiner's Office reported that the buttons on the coat were similar to the button found at the scene of the murder—but its laboratories were unable to analyze the dried blood on the button to see if it matched the traces of blood on the coat. The court released Leonard Goldfaden on a bond of only five thousand dollars, because of the lack of evidence.

The detectives didn't quit. Rogan contacted everyone he could think of, including, he later told me, Nobel Prize–winning scientists. Someone, somewhere, he thought, must be able to analyze the blood on the button and match it with the traces of blood on the coat. Then Deputy Bronx District Attorney Nathan Dembin told his deputies that he had read of my experiments to perfect a technique to reconstitute blood from stains and identify it by sex. Dembin contacted me, and I agreed to help. Rogan flew to Los Angeles with the button and the coat. And I went to work in our laboratory.

I first reconstituted the dried blood from both the button and the coat by combining it with a twenty-percent acetic acid solution in a new process developed by Dr. Hideo Ishizu of Okayama University. Then, in a well-established procedure to determine sex from blood samples, in collaboration with Dr. Omar Alfi, a cytogeneticist, I used a fluorescent microscope with ultraviolet light to examine the reconstituted blood, which had been specially dyed to reveal the chromosome composition of the blood cells. Male blood cells contain an XY chromosome; female blood cells contain an XX chromosome. The dye I used adhered to the Y factor present in the male chromosome but not in the female.

Thus I was able to discover that the blood on Leonard Goldfaden's jacket was the same type as the blood on the button. Even more interestingly, I also found that the blood on both was female and Type O. Leonard Goldfaden had told police that the blood on the lapel of his jacket had come from a fight with a male.

Leonard Goldfaden was brought to trial, and I testified in court that scientific evidence suggested that he was tied in with the murder of a female, his mother. It was the first time such evidence was permitted in a U.S. courtroom. Even though Leonard Goldfaden was convicted, an appellate court later overthrew the verdict because the scientific techniques I had used were too "new."

But I believe that reconstituting blood from dried stains, and typing it by sex, will eventually be established as another tool in forensic science for the capture and conviction of murderers.

THE MOST DANGEROUS GAME

Albert Dekker was a fine character actor who portrayed the suave European in more than a dozen films. But to horror-film addicts he was best known as Dr.

Cyclops, the mad-scientist who shrank his victims into little figures three inches high.

One morning I was in my office when the telephone rang and a police detective informed me that Dekker had committed suicide. I immediately drove out to the actor's Hollywood home, where I found a strange tableau in the bathroom. Dekker had hanged himself in a most unusual way. Vulgar words were written in lipstick on the mirror and on his torso. And he was half suspended by a rope that was wound around his throat and body in a figure-eight fashion, then went over a beam above the bathtub and back to his wrists.

A towel beneath the rope around his throat gave me the first clue that this was not a suicide at all, at least not an intentional one. Then I saw that Dekker was supposed to have been in control of his "hanging," because, although his hands looked as if they were tied, the rope was fixed in such a way that he could release them. What Dekker had created was, in fact, a pulley arrangement with which he could increase the pressure of the rope around his throat and then stop it when he chose. But clearly something had gone wrong.

The actor's body was taken to the Forensic Science Center, and an autopsy revealed that he had indeed hanged himself. But from the other evidence at the scene I concluded that Dekker had not died by suicide. He had died from accidental suffocation.

What had Dekker been doing? I was pretty certain I knew from similar deaths in the past. But to confirm my theory, I called in a consultant to compile a psychological autopsy. Friends and associates of the actor were interviewed about his lifestyle, because we believed that Dekker had apparently been playing the most dangerous sex game in the world.

The strange ritual is known to psychologists as autoerotic asphyxia. And basically it involves hanging yourself for the "ultimate sexual thrill." But the ritualists do not intend to die. Instead they hope to achieve what they believe to be the most sublime sexual experience possible: obtaining orgasm by risking death. Almost always they handcuff themselves, or bind their hands as Dekker had done, and sometimes they wear blindfolds or hoods. Some don transvestite clothes.

Dr. Joe Rupp, Chief Medical Examiner in Corpus Christi, Texas, is an expert on sex-related deaths. In various textbook articles he has discussed autoerotic asphyxia at great length, and he has cited this excerpt from *Justine,* written by the Marquis de Sade in 1791, to show how long the ritual has been practiced:

> We take our stations; Roland is stimulated by a few of his usual caresses; he climbs upon the stool, I put the halter round his neck. . . . Heaven, he himself gives me the sign to remove the stool, I obey; would you believe it, Madame? Nothing more true than what Roland had conjectured; nothing but symptoms of pleasure ornament his countenance. . . . I rush to cut him down, he falls, unconscious, but thanks to my ministrations he quickly recovers his senses.
>
> "Oh Therese!" he exclaims upon opening his eyes. "Oh, those sensations are not to be described; they transcend all one can possibly say;

let them now do what they wish with me, I stand unflinching before Themis' sword!''

Dr. Rupp has also stated that autoerotic asphyxia is astonishingly widespread, ''carried on by thousands of individuals who arrive at this practice independently of one another. It represents an as yet unexplored, almost unknown aspect of human behavior.''

From all appearances, Albert Dekker lost his life playing that dangerous game. Ordinarily, I am reluctant to discuss such sex-related ''curiosity'' cases. But because in Los Angeles County alone some twenty to thirty deaths occur from autoerotic asphyxia every year, and because the practice still seems to be virtually unknown, I believe the public must be made aware of its danger. The truly sad thing is that, unlike the episode described in *Justine*, the ritual is practiced in secret and alone. And if an unexpected accident occurs, death, not the ''ultimate sexual thrill,'' may be the result.

WHEN THE DEAD ROSE OUT OF THEIR GRAVES
Rain pounded the cemetery on a hill overlooking populous Verdugo Hills one morning. A storm had been going on for days, with water pouring into holes made by groundhogs and spreading through their underground network of tunnels beneath the light topsoil until, suddenly, the entire hillside with its cargo of bodies shifted and a mudslide began.

Down toward the city streets slid rotting caskets containing more than a hundred bodies borne on the lip of the mudslide. Within minutes caskets and corpses engulfed the area, plunging through windows into the living rooms of houses, into stores, and lodging against walls. One body ended up wedged in the doorway of a supermarket.

And no one knew what to do. While Verdugo Hills citizens were confronted by more than a hundred ghoulish corpses, Los Angeles bureaucracies fought over which agency should take responsibility (and spend the funds) to redeem the situation.

I heard about the incident a few hours after it occurred and was just as puzzled by the jurisdictional problem. Certainly nothing in the law establishing our office commanded us to take care of bodies that had been buried for years. We were supposed to discover why people died, not why they rose out of their graves. But when another hour passed and I heard that the bodies were still in the houses and streets of Verdugo Hills, I decided to take action and then worry about the legalities.

I drove with my staff to Verdugo Hills. And what I saw there was a scene I'll never forget. Mud had swept the corpses everywhere, some of them now standing grotesquely upright. Meanwhile the pounding rain continued, with water flowing like a river off the hill. But even though I was told that a further mudslide might occur at any moment, endangering our staff, we set to work collecting the corpses.

By that time, other city agencies had decided that if the Medical Examiner's Office had acted without legal basis, they could do so, too. And soon a building in which to store the corpses was found, and we began the process of identification. Most of them, even some buried for decades, were not skeletons, as most people would expect. The skin was gone, but not the muscle and the tissue. And, in a process called adipocere formation, the fat on the corpses had changed to a soaplike texture when the bodies picked up sodium and moisture underground, and their color had become a grayish-white.

Because of the presence of mortuary records and the remains of caskets with labels, the process of identification was not as difficult as in an airplane crash. We first separated the males from the females, and the newer corpses from the older. Then we checked the records for height and age of the deceased. Artifacts and clothing sometimes aided identification. And by the time the rainstorm had ended we were able to return the bodies to the mortuary for reburial.

Whether the citizens of Verdugo Hills have gotten over the shock of that invasion of corpses I don't know. Nor, in all candor, can I be certain that everybody was correctly identified and reburied under the right name. But we did the best we could on that day the dead rose out of their graves.

12

Medical Examiner's Case No. 81-14582

William Holden

The years from 1972 to 1981 were good ones for forensic science. Medical examiners all over the country were growing in prestige and importance, and our work was gaining recognition on several fronts, from the environment to the war on crime.

But slowly and silently a problem was emerging. It began in the late seventies in my state when the citizens of California voted overwhelmingly for Proposition 13, the so-called "taxpayers' revolt" against the ever-escalating cost of government. From that day on, all government agencies, including mine, found it almost impossible to obtain increases in funding even as unexplained deaths in Los Angeles were multiplying. Each year it became apparent that our office couldn't cope with the additional work load. And once again I found myself at loggerheads with the County Board of

Supervisors. Then William Holden's death presented a special problem to me.

It appeared at first as if he had been murdered. Found on November 16, 1981, Holden, clad only in a pajama top, lay on the floor beside his bed in his luxurious Santa Monica apartment overlooking the Pacific Ocean, with a deep gash in his forehead. Blood from that wound had literally soaked the bedsheets and the carpet. But the door to his apartment had been locked, and nothing had been stolen. The police were puzzled. They told the press that Holden had died of natural causes, then shipped the body to the Forensic Science Center for an autopsy.

I supervised his autopsy with sorrow. William Holden had long been one of the motion picture actors I most admired. Born William Franklin Beedle, Jr., on April 17, 1918, in O'Fallon, Illinois, he was the son of a chemist. While he was still young, his family moved to Pasadena, California, where the future actor grew up. At Pasadena Junior College he acted in several radio plays and attracted the attention of a talent scout, who got him a small role in a Hollywood film, *Million Dollar Legs*. He was only twenty-one. He changed his name to Holden, and only one year later he was a major star. His performance in Clifford Odets' *Golden Boy* opposite Barbara Stanwyck won him international fame.

From then on he made more than fifty films. After serving in the war as an enlisted man in the Army Air Force, he returned to Hollywood, to win an Academy Award for his role as an American prisoner of war in *Stalag 17* in 1953, and nominations for his performances as Gloria Swanson's ill-fated lover in *Sunset*

Boulevard and as a television news executive in *Network*.

The titles of some of his other motion pictures have been described as a roll call of Hollywood history: *Our Town, Born Yesterday, The Moon Is Blue, The Country Girl, Picnic.* My favorite of his films was *The Bridge on the River Kwai,* and to me Holden was the actor who most vividly depicted the American male of the World War II generation. It was ironic that I would be accused of denigrating him after death. The truth is, I respected William Holden. But there was a greater truth behind his death which posed the problem.

Several questions formed in my mind as I directed the investigation, including the autopsy on Holden's body. I measured the gash in his forehead that had caused his death. It was two and a half inches long, penetrating the skull. What had caused such a grave wound? And rigor mortis in the limbs of his body and the body's condition, including such surrounding data as body temperature and decomposition, cloudy eyes and a greenish abdomen, indicated that he had been dead at least four days before he was found. How could a world-famous actor with so many friends and business associates die without anyone discovering it for four days? Was that, in fact, a clue to why he had died?

Later in my office, I received the toxicological report and was startled by one finding. Holden had died with .22 percent alcohol in his blood, more than double the .10 percent which is the legal definition of driving under the influence of alcohol by the California

Vehicular Code. Had alcohol contributed to his death in some way? I called Charles Wilson, the chief of homicide detectives in Santa Monica, and asked him if he would join me and my staff in a visit to Holden's apartment.

His apartment seemed to have been inspired by the Hong Kong setting of his film *Love Is a Many-Splendored Thing*. All the furnishings were Chinese, with black-lacquered heavy wood tables, brass-based lamp fixtures and rich Oriental carpets. Holden had exquisite taste in interior decoration. And he was an exceptionally tidy man. Nothing in the apartment seemed out of place—except in the bedroom where he had died.

Charles Wilson had brought another detective with him, and they told me that murder didn't seem to be in the picture. "There were no weapons," Wilson said. "And we dusted for fingerprints. There were none except Holden's in the apartment."

I surveyed the bedroom. One of Holden's fine rugs, oyster white with blue trimming and about three by six feet in dimension, was crumpled near the bed. Such a meticulous man would not have done that intentionally. Had he slipped on the rug? "Where was he lying?" I asked.

"Where the rug is," Wilson said, "beside the bed."

On the bed itself I saw dried bloody Kleenex tissues. I counted eight of them.

The table next to the bed was crooked, another jarring note in such a neat apartment. Apparently it had been jammed at an angle against the wall. In fact, there was a gash in the wall where the corner of the table had struck it. I asked the detective to lift the heavy teakwood table. He couldn't do it. I wanted an idea of the exact weight because it would establish how much force had been applied to move it.

In the kitchen we found an empty quart bottle of vodka in a trashcan, and a partially empty bottle on the counter. I presumed that the contents of those bottles accounted for the .22 percent alcohol reading in the toxicological report on Holden's blood.

From the clues in the apartment, it was obvious to me how Holden had died. Intoxicated, he had tripped on the rug and lunged forward, his forehead striking the corner of the table next to the bed with such force that it had been driven into the wall. His death was an accident. But what made it even more poignant—and pointless—was that the actor had not lost consciousness. Instead, he had opened the drawer of the table in which the Kleenex box was kept, removed some tissues and tried to stanch the flow of blood from the gash in his forehead. He had time to use eight, one after the other.

In the autopsy room, by gauging the amount of blood loss, I had estimated that Holden lived at least half an hour or more before he lost consciousness. And during that time, I suspected, alcohol had played its usual deadly role, preventing him from responding properly to an emergency.

Sober, Holden would probably have telephoned for assistance, or gone next door to alert a neighbor. The telephone was so close to the scene of the accident that there were drops of blood on it. Intoxicated, he lay there on the bed until the blood loss caused him to lose consciousness. And in Holden's case, there was another evil factor at work. Alcohol dilates the capillaries, promoting bleeding, and also inhibits the normal blood-clotting mechanism in an open wound. William Holden bled to death.

Still I had tormenting questions. For one, why had his death gone unnoticed for four days? A woman I knew, Shirley Goldinger, the Director of Consumer Affairs in Los Angeles County, lived next door to Holden, and she gave me a possible answer. Holden was an intensely private person, she said. They had been neighbors for six years, but had only a nodding acquaintance.

Newspaper obituaries of Holden would later make special note of his sense of privacy. All his life he had refused, in interviews, to talk about his politics, his family or his lifestyle. In 1971 he had told a reporter that he had always resented the "ground rule of thirty years ago, when you did anything to get your name in the paper with Hedda Hopper or Louella Parsons."

Such a private person would hesitate before calling for help, I thought. That was probably another factor which led to his death—and also explained why no one was alarmed when he didn't appear in public for several days. No doubt Holden's associates and friends respected his desire for solitude and never bothered him or asked questions.

Bill Martin, the manager of the apartment building, had discovered the body. At my request he joined us in Holden's apartment and told me, "Sure, we were worried. He had been in here for days without coming out."

"How long?"

"I don't know for sure, but it was more than a week. I got concerned, so I played a little game."

I was startled. "A game?"

"Yes—to see how he was doing. I knocked on his door and pretended there was trouble in his electrical wiring. He let me in, and I worked on a light fixture, then told him it was okay and left."

"What did you see?"

"I suspected he had been drinking, but he was okay. Then some days later he was still here, and I was really worried. So I came back."

Standing outside the door of the apartment, he relaxed, he told us, because he could hear the television inside and thought Holden must be all right. But when the actor didn't respond to his knocking, he quickly became alarmed again and used his passkey to open the door.

William Holden perished of a wound which should not have been fatal. There had been ample time to summon help, and even if medical attendants found him unconscious after the summons they could have saved him by modern medical techniques, including blood transfusions. That was why the actor's death angered me. I felt that it precisely demonstrated the terrible danger of alcohol, which is, without doubt, the most popular and most deadly drug ever conceived. One out of every four deaths we autopsy in Los Angeles is alcohol-related.

Holden's death also delineated sharply a great dilemma which faces all medical examiners in this country. Should we tell what we learn from the dead to help the living, or should we try to hide the facts to protect family and friends from embarrassment? I have always believed that our mission is to "tell it like it is." But when I did that in the Holden case, I stepped into an abyss.

The newspaper story which began a professional crisis for me ran on Wednesday, November 18, 1981, in the Los Angeles *Times* under the headlines "HOLDEN DIED FROM BLOOD LOSS. Actor Cut Head in Drunken Fall, Coroner Reports."

The story described my re-creation of the accident, but it was the two words "drunken fall" which started Hollywood talking. Friends of Holden resented it, and they were inflamed even more when the *Times* published a follow-up story on the case which emphasized Holden's alcohol problem: "MANNER OF HOLDEN'S DEATH TROUBLES FRIENDS, FANS." The subhead read: "Rich and Famous, Yet Alone and Intoxicated."

A backlash was perhaps inevitable, and letters charging both me and the *Times* with invasion of Holden's privacy started to arrive at the newspaper, commencing with one from no less a personage than Daryl F. Gates, the Chief of Police. The two *Times* news stories had focused "sharply on a theme that characterized the deceased as a drunken recluse," he wrote. "Bill Holden can no longer defend himself. Without doubt the character assassination is still terribly worrying for his friends and family. In my view what the *Times* did is snooping at its worst."

Another *Times* reader, Theodore Taylor, aimed his wrath directly at me: "The indignity of [Holden's] death was . . . exploited down to the last gory detail by Coroner Thomas Noguchi, who seems to run for his forensic personal publicity kit if the celebrity has passed on in other than a hospital bed."

But a few days later the opposite side was heard

from, in letters written by those who had suffered because of alcohol abuse. A typical writer was Stephen Setzer:

> I am currently in my second week of an alcohol rehabilitation program after fourteen years of misery as a confused alcoholic. . . . I don't agree with the comments of others that [Holden's] state of drunkenness should have been hidden from the public. I feel that if this information inspired even one alcoholic to seek help, it is worth reporting, and that Holden would have wanted it so.

I was caught in the middle of the controversy, a controversy that was aggravated when, only ten days later, a pretty, dark-haired actress drowned accidentally in the rain-swept waters off Catalina Island. My report on Natalie Wood's death caused even more criticism to erupt, and there seemed to be little I could do or say to defend myself or my principles. I thought ruefully that if I were a medical examiner in some remote part of the country the world would have little interest in me or my cases. But I was not. I was in Los Angeles, where, if the bulk of the work of the Forensic Science Center often went unnoticed, headlines erupted when the deaths I investigated were those of world-famous celebrities. Now I was dubbed by the Hollywood wags "Coroner to the Stars." And as if to confirm that description of my work, less than five months after the deaths of William Holden and Natalie Wood another famous star fell into my jurisdiction.

13

Medical Examiner's Case No. 82-3036

John
Belushi

A chilly night on Sunset Boulevard in Hollywood. Young people stood outside the Roxy, a rock 'n' roll bar, waiting patiently to get in. For the attraction that night, March 4, 1982, was not only the music but the presence of three celebrities who were idols to many of America's youth. Robert De Niro, Robin Williams and John Belushi sat at a long table near the stage, laughing and enjoying themselves.

Belushi was considered almost unique as a funny man for his portrayal, among other characters, of the "slob" in such youth-oriented films as *National Lampoon's Animal House* and on the television show *Saturday Night Live*. As he himself once described that character: "He says it's okay to screw up. People don't have to be perfect. They don't have to be real smart. They don't have to follow rules. They can have fun."

Belushi was following such a credo that night—to the hilt.

At 11:15 P.M., a curly-haired young woman pushed her way through the crowded bar to their table. Cathy Smith was carrying a bag which contained, it would later be reported, the "goodies"—drugs. Then, at about 1 A.M., Belushi left the bar, trading jokes with some fans in the parking lot. The manager of the club was worried because he thought Belushi was too drunk to drive, but a "friend" offered to take him home.

"Home" was the Chateau-Marmont Hotel, located on a hill above Sunset Boulevard, its Moorish towers and turrets barely visible through trees which block the view of motorists below. Because it offered a sense of seclusion in the very heart of Hollywood, it was a favorite hostelry for visiting celebrities.

Belushi was staying in Bungalow 3, on the north side of the hotel. On the morning of March 5, he was lying naked on white sheets in the bedroom of the bungalow, curled up on his right side. The room was hot, but he wasn't perspiring. John Belushi, the lovable comic, the carefree "slob," the idol of the young, was dead at thirty-three.

What had happened during the hours of the night after Belushi left the Roxy, laughing and happy? Was Belushi, as his wife insisted, a man who didn't use heroin and, instead, was victimized by a "druggie" one vulnerable night? Or was he, as the LAPD insisted, just another addict who injected himself once too often? Almost all his friends would later add another provocative dimension to the mystery. Belushi was deathly afraid of needles. As his partner Dan Aykroyd said, "Belushi hated even getting his finger pricked for a blood test."

From the viewpoint of forensic science, John Belushi's death would be one of the most challenging in my experience. There were clues I wanted to pursue that might resolve the question of murder or self-injection in his case as well as in other similar ones. But, by coincidence, my own symbolic "death" as Los Angeles County's Chief Medical Examiner occurred on the very morning Belushi's body was found.

That morning I had arrived at the office of Harry Hufford, the Chief Administrative Officer of the county, to discuss the annual budget for the Medical Examiner's department. Instead, I was abruptly informed that the Board of Supervisors had met in executive session and decided that I should resign as Chief Medical Examiner, the post I had held for fifteen years. Hufford said that if I left quietly I would be shifted to another medical position in a county hospital at the same salary.

I told him no.

"Why not, Tom?"

"It's not a *job* to me, Harry," I said. "It's my life."

As I left Hufford's office, it seemed to me that the nightmare of the 1969 Civil Service hearings was about to recur. I walked the broad halls of the County Administration Building numb, feeling nothing. A gray-haired woman saw me and said to her companion, "It's Dr. Noguchi." I pretended I didn't hear her and pressed on toward the pay telephone in the lobby. My face had become recognizable everywhere. And that, I knew, may have been part of the problem.

There was another problem. In the wake of the controversies over the William Holden and Natalie Wood cases, the Los Angeles *Times* had carried a series of articles very critical of me and my management of the Medical Examiner's Office, articles that inspired the Board of Supervisors to launch an investigation of my stewardship. But the forensic scientists whom the Board retained to conduct the impartial investigation had cleared me. Their official conclusion was that I was doing an "excellent" job, considering the well-known shortage of funds and personnel. And at about the same time, my peers had voted me president-elect of the National Association of Medical Examiners. Yet the Board of Supervisors had decided to ask for my resignation.

I picked up the telephone to call my office, my mind still on Hufford's demand. Rita O'Connor, my secretary for thirteen years, answered excitedly. "Dr. Noguchi, John Belushi has died!"

My first reaction was the thought, Just what I need at this point. Holden, Wood and now another famous performer named Belushi—and another media hassle if his death turned out to be controversial. But then I quickly realized I still had a job to do. "Where did it happen?"

"The Chateau-Marmont Hotel. The staff people are just leaving now."

"I'll join them there," I said, and hung up the phone.

Belushi's body was found by William Wallace, a physical therapist, who had shown up at Bungalow 3 at noon for his scheduled massage of Belushi. Wallace immediately summoned a hotel security guard, and the two men moved Belushi to the floor, where they unsuccessfully attempted mouth-to-mouth resuscitation. Medics called to the hotel then employed portable electronic equipment to stimulate the heart, but to no avail. John Belushi was dead.

When police arrived at the scene, they could not figure out what had happened to the actor. His body was unmarked, and there was no indication of a struggle in the room. No weapons were found, no sleeping pills or suicide note, and no drug paraphernalia. In fact, paramedics told police, Belushi's body showed no evidence of fresh needle marks. After observing the lead pads attached to Belushi's chest from the electrocardiograph equipment the medics had used in an attempt to revive him, and the large bulk of the actor's body, police told the reporters clamoring for information outside the hotel that John Belushi had apparently died of a heart attack or choked on some food.

I drove toward the scene along Sunset Boulevard, the old Strip that winds from central Los Angeles to the luxury palaces of the Pacific Palisades. Two centuries ago, it had been a trail for mule trains carrying cargo to and from the ocean; later it was the pathway that motion picture pioneers like Cecil B. De Mille followed from the city to the hills of Hollywood to begin their great industry under the sun. Later still, the hippies had made most of the Strip in Hollywood their own province. Now they were gone, but their spiritual descendants still "owned" the Hollywood section. And along with them, I knew, were prostitutes, hustlers, winos, drug pushers—and murderers.

The murders—and all unexplained deaths—were my prevailing memory of this famous boulevard. How many times had I traveled the Strip racing to the scene of a homicide, from the crowded tenements of the downtown Mexican barrio to the green-lawned estates in exclusive Bel-Air? One day it could be a dope addict, stabbed to death in a downtown alley. The next, a world-famous actress named Marilyn Monroe, a possible suicide. The Strip had led to death for the rich and the destitute alike. Today it led me to the Chateau-Marmont and the body of John Belushi.

A policeman stood behind a barricade across the road that curved off Sunset to the hotel, arguing with reporters who were pleading to get through.

"Any statement, Dr. Noguchi?" they called out to me, thrusting microphones into my face through the open car window. "Was it murder?" "The police say it's a heart attack. Any comment?"

I told the reporters I had no comment and drove up the road to Belushi's bungalow.

My investigation began as I walked past a little fence into the patio in front of Bungalow 3 and looked around carefully. The area was clean and bare. A policeman greeted me at the doorway, then ushered me through a living room into a bedroom on the north side of the bungalow. The decedent lay naked, face up, on the floor beside the bed. I looked at his body from a few feet away, and realized something odd. Belushi appeared to be in his early thirties. It is rare for someone that young to die of a heart attack.

The police had cleared a way to the body, but I surprised some of them when I didn't go directly to it. Others of the LAPD in that room, who had seen me work before, knew my pattern, the first act of what they jokingly called the "Noguchi Show." Instead of crouching to examine the body, I looked up to examine the ceiling.

It is a system of observation at the scene which I've tried to teach young investigators over the years. Don't worry about the body; the body will stay there. (If it gets up, that's another story.) First, examine the room in a systematic, preplanned way, beginning with the ceiling. Clues may be up there: bullet holes, bloodstains, chipped plaster.

Then I began a systematic observation of the walls and the furniture in the room. The ceiling had yielded no clues, but the furniture contained the first bit of evidence. On the nightstand next to the bed I saw a green leafy substance and cigarette paper. Marijuana had been smoked in that room, by either Belushi or others.

But marijuana doesn't kill. I looked elsewhere and saw something unusual on the other side of the room. A little white powder had spilled down the front of the dresser. I walked over to the dresser, a plainclothes police lieutenant following me. Examining the powder, I thought it was cocaine, but I wouldn't know for certain until the laboratory tested it.

In response to my questions, the lieutenant told me that no syringe or drug apparatus had been found in the room, and the medics said there were no needle marks on the body. That's why the police had ruled out drugs as the cause of death.

There was a commotion at the door as my staff, including the chief of the forensic-medicine division, Dr. Ronald Kornblum, arrived. I waited while our photographer snapped pictures of the body from various angles and our investigator took measurements. Then I went to the body and crouched to examine it. Dr. Kornblum and the lieutenant joined me. I saw a little bit of discoloration slightly above the inside of the right elbow. After a moment of thought, I stood up and said, "I believe we have a drug overdose here. Belushi used cocaine—and probably heroin too."

A chorus of voices rose in disagreement, and the lieutenant reminded me that not only had no heroin been found, but no syringe or other drug paraphernalia.

"Then the drug apparatus must have been removed," I said.

"But there aren't any needle marks," one of my staff said.

"We'll have to wait until the autopsy to find out if there are needle tracks," another staff member commented.

"Not necessarily," I said, to the surprise of my staff —and the police. "We may be able to tell right now."

Crouching again beside the body, I gripped Belushi's upper right arm with both of my hands, then squeezed.

Nothing happened.

Again I pressured the upper arm while everyone watched. Suddenly a tiny drop of blood appeared at the inner elbow. A murmur went around the room. There *had* been a puncture in the skin, additional confirmation of my theory that very probably Belushi's death was drug-related.

I repeated the squeezing process on the left arm, and again a tiny drop of blood emerged. Now I knew there was no question. Belushi had overdosed, probably with a speedball, a combination of cocaine and heroin.

But the very fact that the fresh punctures had been so difficult to discover worried me. Apparently a tiny medically clean needle had been used, and the injections had been made right into the vein, so that only drops of blood revealed them. Belushi was obviously not a routine drug addict with a scarred arm. I thought it possible that he might have been injected by someone else.

"The real question in this case isn't whether Belushi overdosed," I said to the police lieutenant, "but whether someone else injected the drugs into him."

I could not yet be certain, of course, but I knew that my question would create a dilemma for the police. If someone else had injected Belushi, that act could be legally defined as murder. But it was the most difficult of all crimes for which to gain a conviction. And when the drug and its apparatus were absent, as they were in this case, conviction was even more difficult. In fact, even if the apparatus was returned later, such tests as fingerprint identification would be hampered because it had been handled after the crime. So it appeared that if my theory was correct there would be no tangible evidence to prove it.

Almost everyone believes it is impossible to determine whether a person has injected himself or whether someone else has inserted the needle into the veins of his arms. I believe that a forensic expert can discern the difference.

My theory begins with the fact that the human body,

forensically speaking, is a skeleton with hinges. For example, in the arm there is a hinge at the elbow and another at the wrist. These hinges are not universal joints. They can move only certain ways. So if one administers an injection to himself, holding a syringe with the thumb and the index and middle fingers, a certain type of puncture will be made. It is called a "signature," and it involves not only the location of the injection but also its direction.

Such a signature is something that cannot be copied easily by anyone else, because one finger may be a fraction of an inch longer or shorter, one skeletal hinge smaller or larger. Also, the muscles in the index and middle fingers are characteristic of the person making the signature. That's why each injection is unique.

Forensic scientists can thus compare fresh puncture wounds with old ones to see whether they reveal a different signature from the subject's normal pattern of punctures, again not only in location but, more important, in the direction of the injection. To illustrate, if you hold out your left arm and pretend you are injecting it with a syringe held in your right hand, you'll observe that the needle will enter the vein at an angle from the right side. But if another person injects the needle into your left arm, he will almost always do so straight up the vein, not from a right angle.

About an hour after my staff and I left Bungalow 3 at the Chateau-Marmont, a car pulled up to the scene and a young woman named Cathy Smith got out. She gave the police a syringe and a bent spoon with a scorched underside and said it was the drug apparatus that had been used the night before, which she had taken with her when she left the bungalow.

Cathy Smith would later tell a *National Enquirer* reporter that she had administered the coup de grâce to Belushi. Later still, she would deny the story and threaten to sue the newspaper.

Belushi's death was ruled accidental, but his widow, Judith Jacklin, would launch a battle to have a grand jury investigate the circumstances. The jury would indict Cathy Smith for second-degree homicide.

However, the very day after Belushi died I was once more embroiled in my own life-and-death career struggle. Dr. Kornblum performed the autopsy, which confirmed my theory that he had died of a drug overdose. But because of my legal problems I wasn't able to follow up on my scientific theories involving the "signature" of the injections that had killed him. I've had no connection with the case since and don't know what role the Medical Examiner's Office played in the indictment of Cathy Smith.

14

Coroner on Trial

On the evening of November 12, 1982, in Newport Beach, flares in the garden of the Newporter Inn burned on brass poles with reflectors that created little pools of heat which warmed the crowd gathered there. Medical examiners were assembled from the four corners of the United States for their annual convention. We were attending the cocktail party that preceded the banquet at which I would be installed as president of the National Association of Medical Examiners.

It had been quite a week for me. On Wednesday I stood in a courtroom listening to my attorney make his closing remarks in my Civil Service battle to retain my job. The very next day I was in Newport Beach participating in the convention whose climax would be my installment as its head.

As I moved through the crowd greeting friends, my

whole life seemed to flash before my eyes like a speeded-up film. For there was Dr. Bill Eckert, large and genial, whose wisdom I had requested in the Robert Kennedy case. There was Dr. Robert Litman, the psychiatrist on the suicide panel in the Marilyn Monroe case. There was Dr. Joseph Choi, who had performed the autopsy in the Natalie Wood case. And all around were medical examiners who had flown to Los Angeles earlier that fall at their own expense to testify for me at my hearing—Drs. Bill Sturner of Rhode Island, George Gantner of St. Louis, Ali Hamili of Wilmington, Delaware, and others from all over the country.

Had their efforts been in vain?

My current ordeal had begun when, two days after Christmas 1981, the Los Angeles *Times* published the series of articles critical of my office and of me. In an interview, I had told *Times* reporter Laurie Beckland that I graded myself only a seven on a scale of ten as a manager, a modest assessment, I thought. But the title of her story reporting the interview read: "Noguchi's Ego Seen as Single Flaw," and her first paragraph prefaced a discussion of my managerial "problems" with these words: "If you could get two people to agree on anything about the controversial Dr. Thomas T. Noguchi, who is often called 'Coroner to the Stars,' it might be that he is a dedicated, imaginative scientist with a single flaw." And that flaw was "variously described as 'ego,' 'ambition' and 'the need always to be the big cheese.' "

Dr. Noguchi, the story went on, "contends he has channeled his ego into a 'driving force that makes this department distinguished from others.' '' But Beckland found ex-employees such as Dr. Ahmed Eid, a toxicologist, who said, "Dr. Noguchi is OK as a coroner when he puts his head to it. But he's worried about political stuff, to be on TV, to be well-known, to be famous. And everything in his office is directed to that."

I could not deny the ego charge, because I was proud of my accomplishments. It had been difficult to come to this country, hardly understanding the language, and rise to a position of scientific prominence. But "fame" had come to me, not because I sought it, but because the victims who died in my jurisdiction were world famous and the press subjected me and my office to close scrutiny in those cases.

Perhaps because of my Japanese heritage, I do have a sense of ceremony—and in America that's called "showmanship." I admit it's an aura which seems to surround me, no matter what I do.

But Beckland's charges had not stopped there. Once again, I was accused of talking too much about the Holden and Wood cases. And, far worse, her story stated that I mismanaged my office, that police evidence and decedents' property were routinely lost or misplaced, that bodies were "stacked" on gurneys. In short, she claimed I had created a chamber of horrors in the Los Angeles County Forensic Science Center.

The public was stunned—justifiably, if those charges were true. And the Board of Supervisors had moved quickly to appoint an investigating panel to audit my management of the office—to find out, as Supervisor Michael Antonovich would later state, whether the *Times* charges were "fact or fiction." As part of the audit, Leslie Lukash, M.D., Chief Medical Examiner of Nassau County, New York, was added to the panel by the Supervisors to head an impartial forensic investigation of my office. When it was completed, Lukash stated as his official conclusion: "Dr. Noguchi and his staff are doing an excellent job in operating the medical examiner's office after recognition is given to the resources available to him at the present time."

There, I thought, the matter would end. But, contradicting its own impartial experts, the Board of Supervisors asked for my resignation. When I refused, I was demoted out of the department, and I prepared, once again, to battle for reinstatement.

In the fall of 1982, at a Civil Service hearing presided over by Sara T. Adler, Godfrey Isaac, my never-say-die attorney, handled my defense along with his partner, Rosalind Marks. As in 1969, the case made front-page headlines and the hearing room was crowded with reporters and curious spectators. But Isaac had warned me that the outcome might not be as favorable as in 1969. For the real source of most of the charges against me was invisible and could never be called to testify. The ghost of Proposition 13 haunted that hearing room.

Often while I sat there listening to the county witnesses testify against me, I thought back to that wonderful day in 1972 when the Forensic Science Center had opened, filled with glistening new equipment and staffed by experts. In those days I had viewed the future as limitless: we could do our job and at the same time expand the frontiers of our fledgling science. What had happened since? The tide of homicides and unexplained deaths in Los Angeles had doubled, tripled, quadrupled. But the staff had not expanded to cope with the work load. And the equipment, new in 1972, was now ten years old and in need of repair or replacement. We couldn't obtain the money to maintain it efficiently, or to purchase new equipment when our 1972 devices became outmoded.

It was ironic, I thought, that as soon as I was demoted out of the office the County Board of Supervisors had appropriated new funding of almost one million dollars to the Forensic Science Center and approved the hiring of an approximate fifteen percent increase in personnel. I was never given a chance to run the office with that new funding and personnel.

Dr. Joseph Choi, a distinguished pathologist who had been promoted to assistant chief of forensic medicine, testified in my behalf and painted a vivid picture of conditions at the center before the infusion of new funds. Wasn't it true, William Masterson, the private attorney for the county counsel asked him, that there were deficiencies in the Medical Examiner's Office?

"We were overworked," Choi said, "working with crippled equipment, working by hand. We could not give the best service to the county. Our hands were tied."

Then, his voice rising sharply in indignation, Choi continued, "I remember times in the bloody autopsy room we did not have paper towels for two or three days. Not even paper towels. Can you imagine that?" He paused, then asked Masterson, "Do you work with bloody hands?"

"Can we get out of the autopsy room, please?" Masterson said uncomfortably.

Because of the shortage of staff, we also had storage and filing problems at the center, but Arleigh Macree, head of the LAPD's firearms and explosives unit, a detective with eighteen years' experience, responded to the charge that we were careless with items of evidence. As he took the witness stand he startled the hearing with his first words: "I'm the only bomb technician available in the LAPD at this hour, so if my beeper goes off I'm going to have to leave."

Macree then informed the hearing that his unit "probably takes more evidence out of the coroner's office than any other in the LAPD. We have contact almost on a daily basis." He said that "most homicides are committed with firearms. Around eighty percent. Therefore we're going to take about eighty percent of the evidence handled by the coroner's office."

And how had Dr. Noguchi's office done its job?

"It's been superb," Macree said. Then he exploded his own bombshell. "In fifteen years, I've never known them to lose one item of evidence." And he added, "I found the coroner's records impeccable."

Ironically, the charge which had inspired the *Times* series, my "needless" statements after the deaths of such celebrities as Natalie Wood and William Holden, was hardly touched upon by the prosecution. But Dr. Cyril Wecht, formerly the Allegheny County, Pennsylvania, coroner and a past president of the American Academy of Forensic Science, spoke on the subject of what a medical examiner can or should comment on after deaths. Testifying in my behalf, he said, "Well, I know of no impermissible areas by statute or even by tradition or custom. I can't think of anybody ever telling me what I could or could not say . . . I always felt constrained as a coroner to divulge information and to share it with the public through the news media . . . if I felt there was a legitimate interest and concern."

The cause and manner of death, as well as the circumstances surrounding it, he continued, are "matters of public record." And, concluding, he said, "I think it is the duty and responsibility of the . . . medical examiner to share information, especially information that might be of public interest and concern."

When the hearing ended, many observers felt I had clearly won my case on the evidence. But I believe I was the only one who thought I had a chance of actually winning the decision. The specter of the *Times* articles still cast a terrible shadow. And the testimony, in my favor, of such law enforcement officials as Detective Macree, as well as my peers and employees, had received little media attention.

And so I waited.

From my apartment in Marina Del Rey, overlooking the ocean, I could see the great waves crashing up and down the beach during the savage storms that, day after day, assaulted the California coastline in the winter of 1983. My career had been like those waves, I thought: an unpredictable succession of highs and lows. The strain had told on my domestic life. After a long separation, Hisako and I were divorced in 1982.

Yet between the lows my life had been a personally gratifying adventure in science. And as I faced an uncertain future I often pondered the past. I thought most often of the Forensic Science Center, and of the brash predictions I had made to reporters at the time of its dedication over ten years ago. Had any of them come true?

Yes, they had. The center had long been cooperating with other medical authorities in a program to aid patients who needed organ transplants. And as an essential adjunct to the program, California now had a law that established a precise definition of brain death. Otherwise, for example, a murderer might say, "I shot the man but I didn't kill him. The doctors killed him when they removed his heart."

There was also a law that required, in addition to testing the alcohol level in the blood of deceased drivers, mandatory testing for barbiturates and amphetamines as well. Our office had been instrumental in its passage as part of programs to prevent the abuse of alcohol and drugs. The more evidence of drug involvement in unnecessary deaths, the more pressure can be brought to bear to combat drug abuse.

Our office had also helped establish guidelines for the termination of life-support systems in cases of irreversible brain damage. And by law the jurisdiction of the Medical Examiner's Office now extended to cover not only private nursing homes but also mental hospitals, where many suspicious deaths occurred, mostly stemming from abuse of patients by staff attendants.

Another law we wanted passed sprang from a tragedy in a hospital. A new surgical wing had just been dedicated, but the very first surgery in it ended in disaster. A patient was given anesthetic and turned blue. When the anesthesiologist administered oxygen, the patient turned bluer and died! Our office was called in, and an autopsy showed that the anesthetic, pure nitrous oxide, filled the victim's lungs. No oxygen.

We learned from our anesthesiology consultant that oxygen is normally given to the patient along with the nitrous oxide because the body can't tolerate nitrous oxide without it. So both gases are piped through the wall. The nitrous-oxide pipe is blue, the oxygen pipe green; they are color-coded to prevent the anesthesiologist from making a mistake. As a final precaution, the connecting heads of the pipes are designed so that they don't match. What had happened? Someone working in the new construction had seen that the pipe heads didn't match, and rigged up an adaptor to connect them. The result was that nitrous oxide was pumped through *both* pipes—and the victim received a double dose of anesthetic and died.

Because our office wanted to make certain that this would never happen again, we lobbied for a bill which required every doctor's office and hospital to conduct a periodic anesthetic-sample certification. But the proposed bill met with howls of protest from the California Hospital Association, the Dental Association, the State Department of Health and other medical agencies.

I remember one telephone call: "Dr. Noguchi, we have thousands of dental offices in the state. This is monumental work for us."

Finally it was suggested as a compromise that the State Department of Health would promulgate a *rule* requiring sampling, but the state would not enact a law. State Assemblyman Paul Banai, the author of the law, concurred. And our office went along with the compromise because we knew we had achieved our purpose. We had alerted all of the relevant medical agencies, associations and hospitals to the problem, and they would be much more careful in the future. In fact, no such tragedy had occurred since.

I was proud of the work we had done at the Forensic Science Center in the past and was determined to continue to be an outspoken voice for forensic science in the future, whatever happened in my own career. Finally, on February 10, 1983, hearing officer Sara Adler was ready to announce her decision, which, in effect, would be her recommendation to the Civil Service Commission. I stood in the hearing room that day as Adler's decision was handed to Isaac and me.

On the basis of the evidence she had heard during the months-long trial, Adler ruled that I had been *unjustifiably demoted*. She stated that I had never been given the chance to show whether I could manage the department with the new funds and personnel which had been granted only after I left.

It was the happiest day of my life. I had won my battle for reinstatement.

But from the high elation of that moment I plunged to another low. On February 23, the Civil Service Commission voted to disregard Adler's recommendation, rendering, in effect, the hearing that had lasted for months and cost the county hundreds of thousands of dollars a farce. The commission said that her findings did not justify her conclusions—that in the course of her report she had implied that I was not a good manager.

I am appealing that decision, and in doing so it is sometimes easy to feel sorry for myself, to believe that

I have been the victim of bureaucratic harassment or even of some kind of personal vendetta. But, along with almost all of my fellow medical examiners, I have come to realize that I may be only a symbol—that my demotion really represents a bureaucratic fear of the independence of the medical examiner/coroner, whoever he may be. But it is precisely that independence that must be protected and preserved. A medical examiner serves to protect the people. When death strikes, inadequately trained or unscrupulous doctors or incompetent, corrupt or simply careless policemen may be present at the scene. It was precisely for this reason that laws were enacted to make the medical examiner the official in charge of death investigations.

Forensic scientists, whether they are public officials or not, are the guardians of society. Our mission is to protect life through the lessons we learn from death. It is a noble crusade, and I am happy to have played a part in its growth. Once, during the early days of my battle to regain my job, I was asked to appear on a local television station to tell my side of the story. Before the interview, a secretary in an outer office handed me a short form to fill out. Under job title I wrote "Fighting Coroner." That bit of bravado was picked up by the newspapers, and I found I had created a new image for myself, far preferable, in my opinion, to the old epithet "Coroner to the Stars." So my present struggle is both a personal battle and a crusade for forensic science itself. There's a sign on the door of my current office in the Los Angeles County–USC Medical Center. It says, "Welcome to Siberia." I've drawn a little smiling face on it.

About the Authors

THOMAS NOGUCHI was born in Japan and came to the United States in 1952 to complete his residency in pathology at Orange County General Hospital in California. In 1960 he joined the Los Angeles County Coroner's Office as Deputy Medical Examiner, and subsequently was appointed Chief Medical Examiner. After he left that post in a storm of controversy, his professional colleagues elected him President of the National Association of Medical Examiners.

JOSEPH DIMONA began his writing career on the *Washington Post.* In 1976 he was awarded the New York State Bar Association Prize for the best legal reporting of the year for his *New York* magazine case study on the John Mitchell–Maurice Stans trial. His books include the best-selling novels *Last Man at Arlington* and *The Benedict Arnold Connection,* and with H. R. Haldeman, *The Ends of Power.* Mr. DiMona is a lawyer and member of the bar of the District of Columbia.

Private Lives of Very Public People

___CORONER Thomas T. Noguchi, M.D. 54088/$3.50

___THE BEAUTY AND THE BILLIONAIRE
Terry Moore 50080/$3.50

___LANA: THE LADY, THE LEGEND, THE
TRUTH Lana Turner 46986/$3.95

___STREISAND: THE WOMAN & THE LEGEND
James Spada with Christopher Nickens
45523/$3.95

___A MAN OF HONOR: THE AUTOBIOGRAPHY
OF JOSEPH BONANNO Joseph Bonanno
with Sergio Lalli 50042/$3.95

___EVA EVITA: LIFE AND DEATH OF
EVA PERON Paul Montgomery 45364/$2.95

___MAX PERKINS: EDITOR OF GENIUS
A. Scott Berg 46847/$5.95

___VIVIEN LEIGH Ann Edwards 55220/$4.95

___STAND BY YOUR MAN Tammy Wynette
45849/$3.50

___MINNIE PEARL: AN AUTOBIOGRAPHY
Minnie Pearl with Joan Dew 43536/$2.75

___SING ME BACK HOME
Merle Haggard with Peggy Russell
55219/$3.95

___THE IMPERIAL ROCKEFELLER:
A BIOGRAPHY OF NELSON A. ROCKEFELLER
Joseph E. Persico 47146/$3.95

POCKET BOOKS, Department BIO
1230 Avenue of the Americas, New York, N.Y. 10020

Please send me the books I have checked above. I am enclosing $_____
(please add 75¢ to cover postage and handling for each order. N.Y.S. and N.Y.C.
residents please add appropriate sales tax). Send check or money order—no cash
or C.O.D.'s please. Allow up to six weeks for delivery. For purchases over $10.00, you
may use VISA: card number, expiration date and customer signature must be
included.

NAME _____

ADDRESS _____

CITY _____ STATE/ZIP _____

☐ Check here to receive your free Pocket Books order form.   437

Home delivery from Pocket Books

Here's your opportunity to have fabulous bestsellers delivered right to you. Our free catalog is filled to the brim with the newest titles plus the finest in mysteries, science fiction, westerns, cookbooks, romances, biographies, health, psychology, humor—every subject under the sun. Order this today and a world of pleasure will arrive at your door.

POCKET BOOKS, Department ORD
1230 Avenue of the Americas, New York, N.Y. 10020

Please send me a free Pocket Books catalog for home delivery

NAME _____

ADDRESS _____

CITY _____ STATE/ZIP _____

If you have friends who would like to order books at home, we'll send them a catalog too—

NAME _____

ADDRESS _____

CITY _____ STATE/ZIP _____

NAME _____

ADDRESS _____

CITY _____ STATE/ZIP _____

368